Understanding community penalties

CRIME AND JUSTICE
Series editor: Mike Maguire
Cardiff University

Crime and Justice is a series of short introductory texts on central topics in criminology. The books in this series are written for students by internationally renowned authors. Each book tackles a key area within criminology, providing a concise and up-to-date overview of the principal concepts, theories, methods and findings relating to the area. Taken as a whole, the *Crime and Justice* series will cover all the core components of an undergraduate criminology course.

Published titles

Understanding youth and crime
Sheila Brown

Understanding crime data
Clive Coleman and Jenny Moynihan

Understanding white collar crime
Hazel Croall

Understanding justice
Barbara A. Hudson

Understanding crime prevention
Gordon Hughes

Understanding violent crime
Stephen Jones

Understanding community penalties
Peter Raynor and Maurice Vanstone

Understanding criminology
Sandra Walklate

Understanding community penalties
Probation, policy and social change

Peter Raynor and Maurice Vanstone

Open University Press
Buckingham · Philadelphia

Dedication to the memory
of David Sutton

Open University Press
Celtic Court
22 Ballmoor
Buckingham
MK18 1XW

email: enquiries@openup.co.uk
world wide web: www.openup.co.uk

and
325 Chestnut Street
Philadelphia, PA 19106, USA

First Published 2002

A catalogue record of this book is available from the British Library

ISBN   0 335 20626 3 (hb)   0 335 20625 5 (pb)

Library of Congress Cataloging-in-Publication Data
Raynor, Peter.
    Understanding community penalties: probation, policy, and social change/
Peter Raynor and Maurice Vanstone.
        p. cm. — (Crime and justice)
    Includes bibliographical references and index.
    ISBN 0–335–20626–3 — ISBN 0–335–20625–5 (pbk.)
        1. Probation – Great Britain.   2. Community-based corrections – Great
Britain.   I. Vanstone, Maurice.   II. Title.   III.   Crime and justice (Bucking-
ham, England)

HV9345.A5R393 2002
364.6′3′0941 — dc21   2001059324

Typeset by Type Study, Scarborough
Printed in Great Britain by St Edmundsbury Press, Bury St Edmunds, Suffolk

Contents

Series editor's foreword

This book by Peter Raynor and Maurice Vanstone is the latest contribution to the Open University Press Crime and Justice series, which provides relatively short but challenging textbooks on important areas of debate within the fields of criminology, criminal justice and penology. All the books are written by experienced lecturers and researchers, and the aim is to give undergraduates and graduates both a solid grounding in the relevant area and a taste to explore it further. Although aimed primarily at students new to the field, and written as far as possible in plain language, the books are not oversimplified. On the contrary, the authors set out to 'stretch' readers and to encourage them to approach criminological knowledge and theory in a critical and questioning frame of mind.

The focus in this volume is on 'community penalties'. This covers broadly those sentences of the court which involve some form of supervision or intervention by the probation service, and much of the text focuses on the work of this key criminal justice agency. Both authors are not only distinguished academic writers, but were formerly probation officers. Their work consequently offers an effective combination of theory and practice. It is also right up to date in terms of developments in the field.

Raynor and Vanstone provide important insights into the changing face of probation as penological thinking and how the politics of criminal justice have shifted over time. They show how, in evolving from a voluntary supplier of charity to ex-prisoners into a major professional organization, the probation service in England and Wales – as in many other countries – has undergone many 'makeovers' and has made a wide variety of claims about its core role and the special expertise of its officers. These include 'advising, assisting and befriending' offenders, providing 'treatment' or 'rehabilitation' and, currently, assessing and managing risk, delivering 'community punishment' and running carefully designed 'offending behaviour programmes'. At other times, especially during the 1980s, it has seen its role primarily as one of 'limiting damage', through advocating 'radical non-intervention', or attempting to 'divert' offenders from prison by attempts to persuade sentencers to place them under community supervision.

Most previous writers on the subject have discussed such shifts at the level of changes in criminal justice rhetoric and fashion, and some have traced their connections with much wider social changes – latterly, the major upheavals associated with 'late modernity'. Raynor and Vanstone provide a good summary of these arguments, but also add the important and often neglected dimension of changes in *practice* – in how probation officers have adapted their actual day-to-day ways of working with offenders as major changes in penological and political rhetoric have swept over the organization.

Another important contribution of the book is the insight the authors offer into the so-called 'What Works' research in Canada, the US and the UK, evidence from which has played a major part in the recent revival of optimism that large numbers of offenders can be 'rehabilitated' through interventions by probation officers – a revival, indeed, that has done much to rehabilitate the probation service itself (in the early 1990s in England and Wales, it should be remembered, it lost the confidence of politicians and came close to extinction as an organization with claims to professional expertise). Raynor and Vanstone themselves contributed substantially to this research, which brings valuable knowledge and experience to their account.

Other books already published in the *Crime and Justice* series – all of whose titles begin with the word 'Understanding' – have covered penological theory (Barbara A. Hudson), criminological theory (Sandra Walklate), crime data (Clive Coleman and Jenny Moynihan), youth crime (Sheila Brown), crime prevention (Gordon Hughes), violent crime (Stephen Jones) and white collar crime (Hazel Croall). Others in the pipeline include texts on social control, psychology and crime, sentencing and criminal justice, prisons, policing, crime and social exclusion, race and crime, risk and criminal justice, and restorative justice. All are major topics in university degree courses on crime and criminal justice, and each book will make an ideal foundation text for a relevant module. As an aid to understanding, clear summaries are provided at regular intervals, and key terms and concepts are carefully defined. To help students expand their knowledge, recommendations for further reading are given at the end of each chapter.

Mike Maguire
Professor of Criminology and Criminal Justice, Cardiff University

Acknowledgements

A wide range of individuals and organizations have contributed to the development of the arguments and ideas in this book through our contact with them during the several decades we have been associated with the probation service. It is impossible to list them all; however, for their assistance with the historical research thanks are due to Bob Anderson; Roy Bailey; Peter Brice; Brian Caddick; Gerry David; Sir Michael Day; Eirlys Emery; Stan Green; Don Henley; Jan Hill; Denis Hodges; Noel Hustler; Terry Johnson; Keith Jones; Dorothy Lloyd-Owen; David Mathieson; Bob Needham; Chris Noble; Joyce Rimmer; Bruce Seymour; Stephen Stanley and Jill Wheeler.

We owe a particular debt to Gwen Robinson who helped with the index, and to Mike Maguire, the series editor, who brought order to our efforts.

chapter one

Introduction

Probation, rehabilitation and socio-political change
Some new directions
Structure of the book
Further reading

This book is about 'punishment in the community', a term which first came into vogue in Britain during the late 1980s as part of an attempt to reposition or rebrand the supervision of offenders in the community (see, for example, Home Office 1990b). The work of probation officers in supervising offenders on probation orders had not previously been seen explicitly as punishment, but as a form of conditional liberty, an expression of the court's mercy in a deserving case, or a form of social work with offenders to help them overcome personal difficulties linked with offending. Legally, before 1991, a probation order was an alternative to sentencing rather than a sentence in its own right. Until 1997 it required the consent of an offender before the court could make the order, so that an explicit agreement or contract with the probationer formed the basis of the supervisory task. Although such consent might be somewhat artificial, or represent a forced choice for the offender who feared he or she would otherwise go to prison, many practitioners and commentators attached at least a symbolic value to it, and it helped to distinguish the probation order from a straightforward imposed punishment.

Other forms of supervision were similarly unlikely to be seen as simply punitive: the supervision orders for juvenile offenders created by the 1969 Children and Young Persons Act were part of a framework which intended court orders to assist in the development, maturation and welfare of children in trouble, and although not removing juveniles altogether from the criminal court system, as is the case with the Scottish children's panels (see Smith 2000), the juvenile justice system of England and Wales was clearly influenced by the same climate of opinion (Home Office 1968). On the other hand the community service order, introduced in the early 1970s for adult offenders and administered with considerable initial misgivings by the probation service, was not primarily designed to assist offenders, but instead required them to undertake a specified number of hours of unpaid work for the general benefit of the community. This looked more like a punishment, and was often described as a 'fine on time', but arguably involved a fundamental difference from conventional forms of punishment in that it required the active participation of offenders and involved a form of reparation to the community.

In addition to these core disposals, the British community supervision system of the 1980s contained a variety (to offenders, perhaps a bewildering variety) of initiatives that were hard to classify as straightforwardly punitive, ranging from day training centres (Vanstone 1993) to 'new careers' (Seddon 1979) and groupwork-based or adventure-based 'Intermediate treatment' (Thorpe 1978) for juveniles. While all of these, like probation and community service, whether or not they were recognized as such by probation officers and social workers at the time, were undoubtedly *penalties*, since they were requirements or restrictions imposed by courts as a consequence of a crime, it is by no means so clear that they were all *punishments*. This book is an attempt to describe how and why the supervision of offenders in the community emerged and developed as an integral part of the criminal justice system, and how and why, more recently, it has come to be seen as punishment. We also explore whether this is now the best or most productive way to understand it, and consider some current and future options for its development.

This book also marks, for the authors, the latest stage in more than 30 years of thinking about these questions, first as probation officers trying to make sense of our daily work, then later as teachers, trainers, managers, researchers and writers. Our previous writings have reflected the particular preoccupations and tensions of the times when they were produced: for example, the preoccupation of the early 1980s with alternatives to custody and coercive 'treatment' and the search for negotiated contracts with offenders under supervision (Raynor 1985); the opportunities we saw for effective practice by probation services when the 1991 Criminal Justice Act combined a 'just deserts' approach to sentencing with a clear intention to reduce imprisonment (Raynor *et al.* 1994); and a strong warning not to neglect issues of social context, social justice and social need as the process of supervision increasingly sought to focus simply on offending (Drakeford and Vanstone 1996). Often our thinking has been stimulated by periods of optimism, when new legislation or new technical developments seemed to offer new opportunities, or imminent political change seemed likely to usher in more enlightened or progressive regimes. At other times, particularly during the mid-1990s, we have found ourselves aligned together with other commentators and researchers in a kind of rearguard action when the potential and future of probation was exposed to the clearest of political threats, as in the 'prison works' campaign launched by the Conservative Home Secretary, Michael Howard, in 1993.

Probation, rehabilitation and socio-political change

This last example points to one of the important underlying themes of this book: the history, development and potential of probation are not simply about what probation officers or probation services can do or want to do. They need to be understood in the context of changing experiences and understandings of crime; social and political changes affecting attitudes to welfare and social needs; changing political and public attitudes; and a more sceptical attitude to the state's role and efficacy in addressing social problems though publicly financed effort. This story has been told in detail, with variations, by several researchers (for example, Garland 1985, 1990, 2000; Bottoms 1995; Feeley and Simon 1992), and we draw on their detailed arguments at several points in the following chapters.

When Radzinowicz (1958: x) made his famous statement that probation was 'the most significant contribution made by Britain to the new penological theory and practice', he was writing in a context of what Garland (1985, 1990) has called 'penological modernism', the belief that crime could be reduced and criminals reformed by the application of scientific understanding and the development of appropriate 'treatments'. The way in which probation developed and was understood for the first seven decades of the twentieth century owes much to these background assumptions, as we show in Chapter 2; and like other attempts to approach and resolve social problems on a positivist 'scientific' basis, it suffered a crisis of confidence in the 1970s, partly as a result of a series of consistently disappointing research findings reviewed in Chapter 4. There were, of course, some negative research findings before the 1970s, and the empirical base for optimism about the effectiveness of probation had never been particularly strong, but it would be naïve to imagine that policy and politics simply reflect the findings of research; rather, research is one of the resources on which policy-makers sometimes draw to support positions which they hold for a variety of reasons. These reasons can include broad social and cultural changes which transform the climate of opinion in a number of interconnected fields.

The weakness of the early research base did not undermine confidence in a 'penal/welfare' approach which was consistent with optimism about the capacity of publicly funded and state-directed welfare systems to reduce and even eliminate a broad range of misfortunes and social problems. In Britain, Beveridge's (1942) report, which laid the foundations of the post-war welfare state, was explicitly aimed at conquering the 'five giants' of want, disease, ignorance, squalor and idleness, with confidence that there were practical methods by which the state could address each of these. Nearly 30 years later, the standard social policy textbooks read by probation officers in training, such as Bruce (1961), still reflected the assumption that welfare states would continue to improve, with increasing public expenditure drawn from economic growth and modestly redistributive taxation. The benefits of enhanced welfare provision were generally recognized, except by a few eccentrics on the margin of politics, and the need for rigorous research to test assumptions about effectiveness was not widely felt. For example, the Seebohm Committee of the late 1960s virtually created the modern social work profession in Britain through a massive reorganization of local authority social services (Seebohm 1968) and also proposed, unsuccessfully, the abolition of the probation service in England and Wales as a separate organization (while this did not come about in England and Wales, the Probation Service in Scotland actually was merged with the new Social Work Departments). Including as it did many of the leading lights of a profession which claimed a scientific basis for its work, the Committee included in its report a chapter on research, pointing out how important it was, and regretting that they had not done any, despite deliberating for two-and-a-half years.

As we now know, and any modern social policy textbook will tell you (for example, Sullivan 1994), the post-war welfare states were not an irreversible achievement, and the culture and assumptions which underpinned them were themselves to be affected by major social and political changes in the industrialized West. Commentators now point out how the establishment of large-scale state welfare reflected the particular social circumstances of post-war reconstruction, collectivist sentiments, wartime experience of central planning, and the capacity of governments to exercise more direction over national economies before the emergence of an international economic order dominated by global corporations (Jordan 2000). During the 1970s, sudden increases in oil prices in response to political and military developments in the Middle East showed how vulnerable the Western economies were, and social programmes underpinned by the expectation of continued economic growth came to be seen as a social burden pushing up tax rates, fuelling inflation and undermining 'enterprise'. The consensus between mainstream political parties about the need for collectivist social provision was undermined by the emergence of a new politics of anti-collectivism which deliberately revived nineteenth-century fears about state welfare provision as a threat to individual freedom and the moral welfare of the poor (Hayek 1944; Friedman 1962; Boyson 1971). In those countries where anti-collectivist political groupings achieved significant power, such as Margaret Thatcher's Britain and Ronald Reagan's America, the changes in sentiment and culture were made particularly clear, but the new scepticism about state welfare services and social engineering spread far beyond these countries and helped to create an audience for negative research findings. Not surprisingly, the same cold wind eventually blew on probation and other rehabilitative enterprises within the penal system.

During the last 30 years in Britain we have seen almost continuous growth in recorded crime; current signs of a reduction in property crime may well, on past form, turn out to be temporary. At the same time, the number of offenders in prison has nearly doubled, from 35,000 in 1971 to over 65,000 in 2001; although this growth is less than the proportionate growth in recorded crime, it represents an increase in the absolute level of reliance on custodial punishment and shows the limited impact of measures designed to reverse its growth. Episodes of severe disorder in the prisons have led to proposals for reform which, under the pressure of increasing numbers and limited resources, have been only partly implemented. It has been argued that the rehabilitative commitment of 'penal modernism' is being replaced by new forms of punishment (Garland 2000) which primarily express public anger or communicate censure. Others have pointed to an atmosphere of 'populist punitiveness' reinforced by political exploitation of public dissatisfaction with criminal justice (Bottoms 1995). Candidates to replace rehabilitation as the underlying rationale of sentencing have included 'just deserts', or punishment proportionate to a moral judgement about the seriousness of the offence (Hood 1974; Von Hirsch 1976); the 1991 Criminal Justice Act claimed this as a rationale, with profound consequences for probation which will resurface throughout the later chapters of this book. This Act actually produced large temporary reductions in the use of imprisonment, until some of its central provisions were reversed as the political atmosphere became more punitive.

Others have suggested that what is actually happening in modern penal systems is not so much about justice as about the management of groups and categories of people perceived as presenting various degrees of risk, and that we are moving towards a system in which offenders will be subject to varying degrees of coercive control on the basis of what they are believed to be likely to do rather than what they have actually done (Feeley and Simon 1992). The use of prison to 'incapacitate' persistent offenders has been described as a return of the 'eliminative ideal' (Rutherford 1997) which lay behind older practices such as banishment or transportation. Meanwhile the government is engaged in a sentencing review which is exploring the possibility of more flexible sentencing based on the characteristics and response of the offender rather than simply on the offence (Halliday 2001) and pursues an uneasy mix of policies based partly on attempts to implement evidence-based crime reduction (Goldblatt and Lewis 1998) and partly on a fear of losing its current electoral advantage by appearing insufficiently 'tough' on crime. This leads it towards policies such as mandatory minimum sentences for repeat offenders and more rigorous enforcement of community penalties which owe more to a political perception than they do to the evidence-based agenda.

The emergence of a victims' movement and its efforts to reverse the criminal justice system's scandalous neglect of victims' rights, needs and perceptions (Rock 1990) have helped to ensure a higher political profile for penal policy issues, and these have become part of the party-political battleground so that policies are developed and enacted quickly if they are seen to have popular appeal, and can be reversed equally quickly if politicians' reading of public opinion requires this. The most consistent recent effort to enact a coherent sentencing system which promised to reduce dependence on prison, the 1991 Criminal Justice Act, was undermined by the repeal of key sections in 1993 before any attempt at a balanced assessment of its impact or effectiveness. As authors we were particularly inconvenienced by this, when our book with David Smith about how probation services could use the 1991 Act constructively (Raynor et al. 1994) appeared just after the Conservative government's U-turn towards a new policy of 'prison works'. Others of course have been inconvenienced much more, including tens of thousands of offenders who have served terms of imprisonment which would not have been imposed under the 1991 Act as originally designed. The search for short-term political returns from headline-grabbing announcements leads to rapid changes in policy with unknown or unintended long-term effects.

Some new directions

In these circumstances it is not surprising that some commentators (for example, Garland 1997) cannot detect any serious challenge to the idea of punishment as a rationale for sentencing. Alternatives have been marginalized and derided as 'soft'. In other areas of social or economic policy, there has recently been an effort to present traditional dichotomies as having been subsumed or made irrelevant by new thinking: not left- or right-wing but 'third way' (Giddens 1998), as the anti-collectivist agenda has itself been discredited and, in Britain, been replaced by the reinvented politics of New Labour. The reinvention has so far stopped short of criminal justice, where the old conflict between welfare and punishment seems to have ended in the hegemony of punishment. We are not offering any glib 'third way' solutions to this, but we believe a careful and sympathetic scrutiny of the past and present of community sentences and 'punishment in the community' can offer some important clues to possible alternatives and promising lines of development. In 1978 John Croft, reviewing what at that time were the disappointing results of research on the rehabilitation of offenders, asked: 'Are these services simply to be abandoned on the basis of the accumulated research evidence? Will the challenge evoke a response . . . by the invention of new approaches and methods?' (Croft 1978: 4). Some of the new theories and methods which have emerged since then offer new and constructive possibilities, and the intense scrutiny of probation and community sentences which has marked the end of the twentieth century and the beginning of the twenty-first has helped to stimulate self-criticism and positive development, however uncomfortable and painful it may also have been.

In our last book (Raynor *et al.* 1994) we argued that the role of probation was not simply to influence offenders away from crime, nor simply to influence criminal justice processes in the direction of more constructive sentencing; instead, it had a dual role, both trying to change the attitudes, circumstances and behaviour of offenders, and trying to promote constructive change in the processes and organizations that determined their fate and shaped their futures. The current quest for credibility and legitimation in community sentences seems also to lie in at least two directions: on the one hand, the increasingly successful search for effective methods of helping offenders to offend less, which goes under the label 'effective practice' or 'What Works'; on the other hand, the development of an effective critical force at the heart of the criminal justice system to challenge the dominance of penal approaches which rely on punitiveness, incarceration, stigma, social exclusion and pessimism about the capacity for change. Recent writing, particularly officially inspired literature such as Chapman and Hough (1998) and McGuire (2000), has tended to concentrate on the first of these two directions, but we will try in our discussion to give some weight also to the second, showing how community penalties might point the way to a more restorative and socially inclusive future for criminal justice.

Structure of the book

In order to achieve this objective we have given some prominence to a historical account of the development of community sentences, because we believe that it sheds considerable light on the questions that need to be answered if that restorative and socially inclusive future is to be attained. We begin, then, by focusing on the origins of the concept of probation and its rise as a prominent community sentence. The subsequent discussion of the role and purpose of community sentences will emphasize the significance of two factors: first, the upsurge of community-based initiatives at the beginning of the twentieth century which shifted prison from its central position in the penal system; and second, the growing pre-eminence of the psychology of the individual offender. In particular, each of these factors will be examined as part of a change which Garland (1985) describes as one from individualism (characterized by separate cells and an interest in uniform punishment) to individualization (characterized by an interest in the identity and motivations of the offender). The chapter will also touch upon the change from charitable and voluntary action to professionalism, and the rise of treatment and rehabilitation as primary criminal justice goals. It will outline the expansion of community sentences from the original probation order to include supervision orders, community service orders, 'combination' orders, post-custodial supervision and the full range of what are called in America 'intermediate sanctions'.

In Chapter 3 the emphasis will be shifted to the theory and practice of community supervision because it is central to our arguments that much of the available history of the involvement of criminal justice agencies in community supervision has been written with a focus on administrative, organizational and legislative history rather than on the nature and impact of the activities of practice. We will, therefore, present a revised account, based on original research carried out by one of the authors, of the development of practice theory and of actual supervision practice in probation services (Vanstone 2001). In so doing, we will explain how practitioners responded to the policy context and the available theories and fashions, what influenced them and how the professional culture of the late twentieth-century probation service was constructed.

One of the features of those practice developments was that they occurred in a relatively unchallenging social and political environment, with relatively little attention paid to evaluating their effectiveness. When that changed in the 1960s, the results of research had the effect of moving the probation service quickly from relative optimism to the pessimism summed up in the slogan 'nothing works'. Chapter 4, then, describes and reappraises this first wave of probation research, including what are now seen to be its shortcomings, and shows how the take-up of the 'nothing works' message was helped by the emerging anti-welfare stance of many Western governments during the 1980s. The impact on practice is discussed (including the emergence of 'diversion from custody' in the 1980s as a more apparently achievable goal than the reduction of offending), and the virtual disappearance of research on the effectiveness of community sentences from 1976 to the 1990s in Britain is contrasted with the different pattern of development in other countries (such as Canada) where research continued. In conclusion, we stress the importance of recognizing the success of many of the 1980s diversion initiatives, and remembering what can be achieved by influencing criminal justice system decision-making.

In Chapter 5 we return to the theme outlined earlier in this chapter, namely the drift towards more punitive criminal justice and greater reliance on custodial sentences during the 1990s in Britain (the process started earlier in the USA). We relate this drift to wider political and cultural changes, and in particular to the anti-collectivist tendency to seek to regulate the poor through law enforcement rather than empowering them through welfare. Our discussion will focus on the penal crisis of the last quarter of the twentieth century, the construction of crime as a political issue and the aftermath of the collapse of the rehabilitative ideal. We move on then to explore the consequent redefinition of community sentences in the 1990s as 'punishment in the community' together with its impact on practice and the development of new forms of accountability and regulation created to ensure the adoption of the new agenda by practitioners.

The rediscovery by politicians and public opinion of a taste for punishment was accompanied by a second wave of research on the effectiveness of supervision which demonstrated that rehabilitative efforts can reduce offending if the right kinds of supervision are offered. In Chapter 6, therefore, we review the current state of this research, drawing on key findings from the UK, Canada, the United States and Australia in order to outline an approach to effectiveness in community sentences. We then provide a context for discussion of current official initiatives to encourage 'evidence-based practice' as part of a wider initiative (by a new Labour government) to reduce crime in society. This part of the book gives an account of the emergence of cognitive-behavioural and pro-social models as methodological expressions of effective practice in offender supervision, and explores the potential of new methods of risk and needs assessment in the planning and evaluation of supervision (drawing on recent Home Office funded research led by one of the authors).

After presenting an overview of the position of community sentences within the criminal justice and penal systems at the end of the century, in Chapter 7 we assess the achievements of and problems facing community sentencing against a background of increased accountability and a growing demand for action on crime. Then we appraise the extent to which community sentences can provide answers to questions posed by both criminological and social imperatives, and the degree to which any such answers might be limited by the criminal justice policy context within which they are sought. Both positive and negative scenarios for future development are outlined, depending largely on whether current tendencies towards bureaucratic punitiveness are emphasized at the expense of the evidence-based and curiosity-driven route to effectiveness. It is our argument in this chapter, first, that a positive and creative vision of the future of community sentences can encompass elements of restorative justice and the social reintegration of offenders as well as offence reduction; second, that the research lessons of the 1990s can be combined with the 1980s emphasis on influencing the criminal justice system; and third, that community sentences can embody a dual focus on influencing offenders towards more pro-social behaviour, and influencing society towards more constructive criminal justice.

We conclude the book by considering the status and position of community sentences within the criminal justice and penal systems at the beginning of the twenty-first century. This necessitates the search for answers to what we believe to be the critical questions facing sentencers, politicians, policymakers and practitioners. How far are existing organizational structures and divisions appropriate for the purposes of punishing and helping in the community those who offend? Is there a case for abolition or reformulation of some existing agencies? To what extent can those implementing community sentences ensure that policy and practice are actually informed by evidence of what is effective in reducing offending and the risk posed by crime to the public? Should community sentences continue to supplement prison or should they (and if so, can they) be used to replace imprisonment in a significant range of cases as the prime method of protecting the public? In our attempt to stimulate further discussion about these questions (providing definite answers is too presumptive), we suggest a future probation service and criminal justice system based on rationalism, evidence-based practice, a sensitivity to the need of offenders to be reintegrated and socially included, and finally, an awareness of the importance, in the age of globalization, of the need for reciprocity in the development of justice and penal policy among different countries.

Further reading

Readers interested in exploring further the subjects covered in this chapter will find a wide range of material among the sources cited, but may find it particularly useful to look at Brownlee (1998) and Worrall (1997). Both provide a succinct overview of the main issues relevant to thinking about the community supervision of offenders.

chapter two

The origins of community sentences

As we asserted in Chapter 1, an understanding of the history of the development of supervising offenders in the community is essential to a full understanding of current policy and practice. Without a grounding in that history we are unlikely to understand (let alone answer constructively) questions facing policy-makers, managers and practitioners at the beginning of the twenty-first century. In this chapter, therefore, we will explore that history in both its orthodox and revisionist forms.

Probation, or the practice of releasing certain people from court with some kind of condition that they behave themselves in the future, is central to the history of community sentences. Explanations for the origins of this practice are as fanciful as they are diverse, and include Athelstane, the Anglo-Saxon king (Home Office 1927, cited in Le Mesurier 1935: 19), Chaucer and the Pilgrim Fathers (Le Mesurier 1935). However, it is America and Britain in the nineteenth century that provide the most promising terrain within which to search for a viable explanation. Both have credible but disputed claims to the invention of the practice of probation, and certainly both contributed significantly to its ultimate form. In this chapter we explore its origins and identify the main forces behind its development from missionary and voluntary work to a fledgling social science. In our account, however, we challenge the orthodox version of those origins, premised as it is usually on the role of probation in an exclusively humanitarian reform movement. Instead, we locate that role within a broader context of psychological, political and religious discourses and histories, and attempt to show that the gestation and introduction of probation was as much to do with maintaining social order and the view of society held by prevailing powerful elites as with helping the less fortunate.

The orthodox histories

The concept of recognizance

Grinnell (1941: 78) proposes that the origin of probation can be found in the case of *Commonwealth* v. *Chase* presided over by Judge Thatcher in the old Municipal Court of Boston. In this case, a woman was acquitted of a further offence while on recognizance,[1] but the prosecutor argued that she should be sentenced for the original offence. Judge Thatcher, who presided in the Boston Court from 1823 to 1843, decided in favour of the prosecutor on the ground that the state had originally retained the right 'to claim judgement' (p. 79). So, as Grinnell argues, by reaffirming the court's continuing jurisdiction over the woman's behaviour, the judge established the legal concept of probation. Technically he appears to be correct, although the connection is rather tenuous, and in fairness he does admit to other possibilities. For instance, in his discussion of the origin of the ideological concept of probation he attributes some significance to the exemption from criminal prosecution claimed by some ecclesiastics, which was later extended in English law to commoners who could prove that they were clerks, namely *benefit of clergy*. Another historian, while acknowledging the fact that a form of recognizance was used in Massachusetts in the seventeenth century, locates its use earlier in England in the sixteenth century as part of the 'general powers granted to the justices of the peace for the prevention of violence and similar forms of misbehavior' (Timasheff 1941: 4).

In Britain in the 1820s the Warwickshire magistrates lay claim to a parallel (and possibly earlier) tradition with their practice of sentencing young people to a nominal day's imprisonment and then releasing them to the care of an employer. It involved no oversight or follow-up, but does seem to draw upon the medieval concept of recognizance, which a number of commentators agree is the legal precursor to probation (King 1969; Jarvis 1972; Bochel 1976; Page 1992; Brownlee 1998). Ayscough (1929), on the other hand, refers to the Continental law of SURSIS[2] involving a conditional sentence. Certainly magistrates in Boston, Massachusetts, seem to have been placing people on a form of probation in the 1830s (Moreland 1941), but, according to Tallack (1984), the process of dealing with the delinquent behaviour of apprentices in the City of London by the chamberlain in his semi-private court pre-dates the system in Massachusetts. Under this system masters could bring unruly apprentices before the court for them to be jailed for two weeks and then released on a promise of good behaviour. However, clearer explanations come from an understanding of the roles of a number of individuals and organizations, and it is to these that we now turn.

The role of Matthew Hill and Edward Cox

In the British accounts, two figures stand out. Matthew Hill and Edward Cox, both recorders in England, used recognizance as a device to give young people the opportunity to reform. In 1841 Hill, a recorder in Birmingham, drawing on his experience in the Warwickshire courts, began the practice of releasing juveniles to the care of people who pledged to act as guardians. The procedure involved the keeping of a register, follow-up by an inquiry officer, and the guardians or parents avowing their responsibilities in a signed declaration (Minn 1950; Bochel 1976). As Hill (1857: 117) himself put it, there had to be 'ground for believing that the individual was not wholly corrupt', and 'that there would be better hope of amendment under such guardians than in the gaol of the county'. Although this was indisputably a second chance, it was circumscribed by limited mercy, and if the juvenile offended again they were guaranteed no further 'indulgence' but rather a more severe penalty (p. 118).

Some commentators argue that Edward Cox, the recorder of Portsmouth and chairman of the Second Court of the Middlesex Sessions from 1870 to his death in 1879, moved closer to the modern concept of probation with his use of a special inquiry officer, recognizance and supervision (Bochel 1976). In challenging this interpretation, however, White (1978) contends that if there was any supervision it was of a very superficial kind. What evidence there is supports White's conclusion, and it is likely that the officer, George Lockyer, confined himself simply to seeking evidence of motivation to reform in those cases where there was some doubt.

The practice, therefore, of releasing people in order for them to prove their good intentions seems to form the core of the emerging idea of probation both in America and Britain between 1820 and the end of the nineteenth century. Timasheff (1941: 1) describes it as a 'social invention' created 'almost simultaneously in Boston, Massachusetts, and in Birmingham, England' in 1841:

> The invention was a new method of treating corrigible offenders convicted of trivial offenses. It consisted in giving such offenders another chance, good conduct after trial being deemed conducive to definite release from punishment, and bad conduct being followed by the imposition of the delayed sentence and by the execution of punishment.

The truth is that each of these competing claims has elements of truth, and there is probably not one single origin. It is not surprising, then, that the accounts contain various and sometimes contradictory interpretations. For instance, within the canon of British histories, the intimacy of the link between probation and the practices of Hill, Cox and the Warwickshire magistrates is in dispute.

John Augustus, the first probation officer?

Bochel (1976) places a much heavier emphasis on the link between probation and the practices of John Augustus, the Boston cobbler, who is generally regarded as the first probation officer. There is little doubt that his work represents a significant chapter in the history of community sentencing. He was an eccentric and notable figure in Boston, rushing around the city in a chaise (Johnson 1928), confounding people with his rapid style of speech (Fenner 1856), and bailing people from court, and then using 'this favor as an entering wedge to the convict's confidence' (Glueck 1939: xvi). Although some challenged his motivation, he was a humanitarian who was committed to the reform of offenders and the disavowal of revenge as a purpose of the criminal justice system (Augustus 1939: 23).

His activities began in 1841 when in court one morning he saw 'a ragged looking man' who told him that if he could be saved from prison 'he never again would taste intoxicating liquors' (pp. 4–5). He persuaded the judge to bail the man to his care, and thus began his practice of putting up a bail surety, helping the person in a number of practical ways and then reporting back to the court at the end of the bail period (Augustus 1939; Glueck 1939; White 1978). Until his death in 1858 he committed himself full-time to the work and stood bail for 1,946 people.

Bochel is correct in her view in so far as Augustus heavily influenced the form that probation took in Massachusetts, which in turn had impact on notable figures in the British reform movement. For example, Howard Vincent MP who introduced the Probation of First Offenders Act 1887 used the American system as part of his argument for the introduction of that legislation. Ruggles-Brise, the Prisons Commissioner and a prominent figure in the pressure for the introduction of probation, visited America and was a strong advocate of their probation system. A Miss EP Hughes who had been Principal of the Cambridge Training College for Women Teachers visited America at the end of 1900 and the beginning of 1901, and subsequently presented a particularly influential report, which the Howard Association published, urging the implementation of the system in Britain (Hughes 1903). Even earlier, according to Muirhead (1914), Joseph Sturge from Birmingham drew attention to the system in Massachusetts in his evidence to the Royal Commission on Reformatory and Industrial Schools in 1883.

The Church of England Temperance Society

Each of these is rightly accorded significance in the movement that brought about the introduction of probation in the United Kingdom. However, it would be a mistake to underestimate the importance of the work of the Church of England Temperance Society (CETS), formerly the Church of England Total Abstinence Society (Harrison 1971), which employed missionaries in general rescue work and the promotion of temperance. In 1872 it shifted its attention to removing the underlying causes of intemperance, and thus aligned itself with mainstream social work (King 1969). Perhaps inevitably, this brought the missionaries into contact with the criminal justice system, but it is the intervention of the Hertfordshire printer, Frederic Rainer, in a letter to his friend Canon Ellison, the Chairman of the CETS, urging the Society to appoint missionaries to the police courts, that most histories identify as a defining moment in probation history. Although the original has not survived (Page 1992), and at least one commentator has cast doubt on its historical authenticity (Osler 1995), it remains an enduring symbol of the humanitarian tradition of most probation histories. The CETS responded with the appointment on 1 August 1876 of George Nelson to the Southwark and Lambeth courts, and in the following year of William Batchelor to Bow Street and Mansion House courts. Between then and the end of the century police court missionaries were appointed across London and other cities and towns, for example, Liverpool and Rochester in 1880, and West Bromwich, Leicester and Worcester in 1884 (Ayscough 1923; Jarvis 1972). In the late 1870s the police court mission involved itself in helping prisoners, a task that had been undertaken by discharged prisoners' aid societies since the beginning of the century (National Association of Discharged Prisoners' Aid Societies (NADPAS) 1956). In 1879 Liverpool was the first of many areas to establish a prison gate mission where prisoners were given a free breakfast, urged to reform and sign a pledge not to drink alcohol (Ayscough 1923). Whether the breakfast was provided before or after they signed the pledge is a frustratingly moot point; it would, indeed, be interesting to know for what it would tell us about the philosophy and techniques of the missionaries.

The work of the missionaries involved informal supervision of people discharged under the Summary Jurisdiction Act, and to this extent Jarvis (1972: 9) is correct in ascribing the role of pioneer of social work to the missionary. However, Bochel's argument that Augustus's system, involving as it did the postponing of sentence, the threat of recall, supervision and reporting, and record-keeping, encompassed most of the features of modern community supervision is the most compelling. How, then, did these activities become ensconced in the legal framework of the community sentencing that was to prevail throughout the twentieth century? The answer is to be found in the small print of the story of political and social reform movements.

The social and political context

At the political level it was the activities of Howard Vincent, a former director of Criminal Investigation at Scotland Yard who had visited Massachusetts and been impressed by what he had seen, that first led to the idea of creating a legal framework for community supervision. He introduced the Probation of First Offenders Bill in 1886, which, because of opposition to his proposal that the police should undertake the supervision, ended up on the statute book in 1887 without any provision for supervision. Much later, in April 1906 according to Ayscough (1929: 71), the CETS in a deputation to the Home Secretary offered itself as the organization to implement a scheme involving 'the appointment by the government of certain officers, called Probation Officers' to supervise adult offenders instead of sending them to prison. Further impetus was given to this idea by the Howard Association, which concentrated a significant proportion of its campaigning effort to this end (Le Mesurier 1935). In their annual reports from 1873 to 1912, probation is a consistently prominent issue. In 1907, then, the Probation of Offenders Act brought to fruition the efforts of the various players in the reform lobby, and ushered in what Radzinowicz (1958: x) would describe as 'the most significant contribution made by Britain to the new penological theory and practice which struck root in the twentieth century'.

It represents the culmination of the idea as described in the orthodox histories and these are imbued with an acceptance of the overriding humanitarian concern of Victorians who, Bochel (1976: 2) maintains, were able to compromise their conception of individual responsibility in the face of the need for reform. Beneath the surface of this concern, however, was a growing anxiety about the moral degeneration of the lower classes (Whitfield 1998). For some, these worries were confined to the earlier part of the century and superseded by the enlightenment associated with people such as Elizabeth Fry (King 1969), and the broader social work project – a project based on rationalism and informed responsibility. It is a point of view re-iterated some 50 years later by a principal probation officer who confidently asserted to a European seminar held in 1952 that the birth of casework was the result of Victorian reformers united in their concern about the conditions in which the poor lived (Paskell 1954).

So, in these accounts the probation project is firmly placed within the humanitarian considerations of those committed to penal reform in the late nineteenth and early twentieth centuries. Their existence is indisputable, but in this chapter, we wish to challenge the weight accorded to them in these accounts. Some more recent accounts have initiated at least a partial challenge, and given more emphasis to the wider context (McWilliams 1983, 1985, 1986; May 1991a, 1991b, 1994; Mair 1997). May (1991b) places what he describes as the 'rising concern at the level of moral degeneration' of a section of the working class, which included 'habitual, drunken and petty offenders' (p. 159), alongside both the utilitarian view that crime is a matter of rational choice, and the efforts made by the criminal justice system to balance deterrence and retribution in order to prevent recidivism. Community supervision was thus handily placed to provide not only an alternative choice for magistrates but also moral training (May 1991a). Explanations for crime were no clearer than they are today, but the dichotomy between eugenicist and environmental explanations was perhaps more stark. Echoing Garland's argument about how the conflicting theories coalesced around the individual as the focus for criminological investigation, May argues that the need for such investigation was given added urgency because this 'soft determinism' cast doubt on the level of individual responsibility in the commission of a crime. Who better, then, to provide clarification than police court missionaries or probation officers. Like McWilliams before him, May too provides an explanation for the subsequent victory of science over religion in the process of the professionalization of the probation officer.

Mair (1997) also touches on this wider context by linking the emergence of probation to a moral panic about drink and its effects and, by implication, a concern about moral degeneracy. However, like May, he stops short of a full revision. McWilliams (1983, 1985, 1986, 1987), who has provided perhaps the most cogent re-examination of probation history, alludes to the eugenicist agenda of some police court missionaries (for instance, he informs us that two prominent figures in the history, Thomas Holmes and Canon J. Hasloch Potter, advocated curtailing the reproduction capacity of the deliberate criminal), and posits his history amidst the harsh socio-economic conditions attended by poverty, drunkenness, prostitution and a spiralling prison population. However, his interest lies in explaining, first, how the police court missionaries, and subsequently probation officers, initially established their position in the courts; and second, how their religious philosophy gave way to scientific explanations for crime (McWilliams 1983). On the first point, he argues that the use of recognizance played a part in stimulating a climate of greater leniency, and produced a conflict for magistrates around the issue of severity or leniency in sentencing. The issue was prominent in debate because in the 1870s and 1880s the cumulative principle (the more court appearances and convictions, the greater the punishment) had contributed to controversially severe sentences. So, McWilliams argues, the missionaries were welcomed in the courts because they created opportunities for leniency and mercy. In turn, these opportunities created a problem of the selection of those who deserved mercy. In other words, through a use of 'common sense and unacknowledged moral evaluation' (McWilliams 1985: 267), the missionaries were involved in the process of deciding who should be saved, and this produced a fatal 'flaw in their ideal' which let in the social diagnosticians. McWilliams asserts that being saved involved the resolution of a drink problem, and that problem, therefore, was a stumbling block to be removed: it was, therefore, determinist. The acceptance of this scientific notion exposed the missionaries to the 'deterministic ontology of the diagnosticians' and a concern with the 'mind and behaviour' (as opposed to the soul) of the offender (McWilliams 1985: 259). Nevertheless, tensions between these conflicting philosophies survived well into the twentieth century and through the era of professionalism. Combined, these later histories contain the religious, social and political elements of a revised version of the history of community supervision, but they fail to achieve a comprehensive and conceptually rigorous account. In the rest of the chapter we attempt to provide that account, and in so doing we need to explain what kind of penal system operated at the time of the development of probation.

A revised account

While recognizance, and later probation, are seen as part of the resolution of social problems (and, to an extent, political and philosophical ones as well), they are less well defined as elements in the competing political, religious and cultural ideologies that constructed definitions of crime and offenders and prescribed those solutions (Young 1976). The concept of community supervision emerged in what Garland defines as the Victorian penal complex, and it developed the version that is familiar to us today, the modern complex (Garland 1985). During the period of the Victorian complex pressure for reform and demand for austere punishments co-existed: concern about prison conditions sat alongside the development of the regime of silence in Coldbath Fields House of Correction, the treadmill and minimal diets (Newburn 1995; Taylor 1998), and concern about rising crime alongside the development of prison as an alternative to capital punishment and transportation (Hudson 1996). Prison, politically favoured as it was, faced competition from only two alternatives: the fine (which often meant prison for non-payment) and release on recognizance. Moreover, offenders were deemed to be in prison as a result of their unconstrained moral decisions. Running parallel to these developments was a revival of philanthropy, symbolized in 1869 by the emergence of social work based on individualization, humanitarianism and the development of professionalism, and, some might argue, by the founding of the Charity Organisation Society (Rose 1961). This aspect of the role of the Society is contentious because it was interested in a scientific version of judgementalism that separated the deserving (a good investment) from the undeserving (a bad investment) and at the same time suppressed mendicancy. Indeed, many branches of the society aimed to reduce grants. Common to both developments, therefore, was a system of classification and the resultant exclusion of groups of people – in particular, those who were undeserving. Although in the modern complex this process became a more scientific one, the notion of the deserving and undeserving informed philanthropic activity, including recognizance and later probation.

From individualism to individualization

During the period of the modern penal complex, from 1895 to 1914, the new interest in the individual (what Garland labels 'individualization') led to the introduction of responses such as detention in reformatorics for the inebriate, detention for the mentally defective, probation and borstal. As a consequence, prison became a sanction of last resort, reformation assumed increasing importance and offenders became objects to be assessed, classified and processed (Garland 1985; Newburn 1995; Hudson 1996). Furthermore, whereas the Victorian complex involved a hierarchy of penalties into which the offender was fitted according to the offence committed and any recognition of mitigating or aggravating factors, the modern complex involved a grid of various penalties to which the offender was matched according to diagnosis. Individualism was supplanted not only by individualization, but also by a regime that assumed the responsibility for reform and applied curative knowledge and techniques in order to control. According to Garland (1985, 1990), the offender, though still constituted as a free and rational subject, was perceived to possess uncertain reasoning and a particular type of personality, the state became the expert and probation moved from religious and moral discourses to those of science and rationalism. It is an acutely observed analysis; however, the story is a little more complicated than it suggests.

Political and public concern about crime and how it was influenced is an important element in understanding the process of penal development and its inherent conflicts as it moved towards probation legislation. What we now recognize as the embryonic modern penal system, with its emphasis on reform and deterrence primarily through prison, was beginning to materialize in the early 1880s. However, in 1856 and 1862, two moral panics about street robbery provoked a backlash against reform, and a Security against

Violence Bill which reintroduced flogging for robbery with violence was hurried through Parliament (Pearson 1983; Taylor 1998). This occurred too early to have any negative impact on the reform that led to probation, but in the context of the history of probation it is important because it exemplifies the complexity of the political and social struggle within the process of reformation during the Victorian period, and it reveals the increasing tendency to conflate concerns about degeneracy and crime. Worry about street robbery was to be subsumed under a more general concern about the degeneracy of a significant proportion of the population. Of course, it is not as straightforward as we imply; there were competing views among powerful elites – for example, in the face of those concerns, environmentalists continued to emphasize the effects of poverty on crime.

The development of probation, Young (1976) argues, has to be located in the midst of this conflict and the need for social order. In his view, 'probation emerged as a policy measure generated out of a relationship between classes in the later nineteenth century' (p. 55), and while the solutions of opposing sides in the argument differed, their underlying motivation to ensure stability in society was the same. The similarity of his arguments to those of Foucault is clear because, while acknowledging that social work had a stabilizing and beneficial effect on the poor, he argues that, like the giving of charity, it was not simply about liberalization and democratization but also about controlling the poor. An essential component of that control was distinguishing between the deserving and the undeserving, and in contributing to this the police court missionaries aligned themselves with ideological stances of middle-class reformers and, moreover, promoted both the acceptance of moral individualism not as an ideology but a self-evident truth, and the accuracy of the middle-class view of society. In Young's view, traditional historical accounts have underplayed this dimension, and the motivations of police court missionaries have been assumed to be humanitarian and not part of any social or political structure. Young's analysis provides a different starting point for a fuller understanding of the early history of probation, but it has gaps which are usefully filled by an exploration of the development of the psychology of the individual, the emergence of eugenics, the role of religion, and social and political concerns about social degeneracy.

The psychology of the individual

Interest in the individual offender lies at the heart of individualization, and is tied inextricably to the psychology of the individual. Individualization is predicated on 'the organic, latent, or manifest criminality of the individual' (Saleilles 1911: 134), and it is to this psychological construction that punishment is adapted. However, the shift from the individualism of the Victorian penal system to the individualization of the modern project presented a dilemma for theorists, politicians and practitioners alike – how could an increasingly deterministic view of behaviour fit the notion of people as responsible moral agents? Saleilles makes an interesting attempt to resolve this dilemma. According to Garland, he produces a classic compromise – what May (1991a) terms 'soft determinism' – and, in so doing, secures the concept of individual responsibility while also promoting both the need for 'a closer study of the complete man, with his distinctive and individual psychology', and 'his participation in the social organism' (Saleilles 1911: 3). He reconstructs this as a more truthful notion of responsibility, which can be applied, but with consideration given to the individual personality and the particular circumstances of the case. This change in the definition of responsibility was prompted, he argues, by a growing awareness that people's life chances were different; in other words, a person's level of moral responsibility might vary according to their state of health, pathology or mental disorder. This idea that a high level of determination equals a low degree of freedom adds weight to McWilliams's (1983) explanation for the succumbing of the missionaries to the scientists because of the 'stumbling block' of drink and the idea that probation was born from the concept of diminished responsibility.

Increasingly, then, the question of what sentence to impose on an offender became an inquiry into the degree of moral freedom exercised in the commission of the offence. The offender becomes Garland's reconstituted subject in the modern penal system, and processes of inquiry separated the deserving from the undeserving. By identifying the deserving, first police court missionaries and later probation officers played a significant part in the segregation and removal from society of the rest. The opportunity for intervention, first by police court missionaries and then by probation officers, is provided by Saleilles' (1911: 181) maxim that '[i]t is the crime that is punished; but it is the consideration of the individual that determines the kind of treatment appropriate to his case'. That process and its emphasis on moral improvement were given impetus in community-based sentences by probation (Glueck 1933).

Throughout its history, probation has drawn its credibility from its purported understanding of the offender and what is needed to change behaviour and attitudes associated with offending. As a consequence, its theoretical and practice base has been inextricably entwined with the story of psychology, and moreover, with its role in the processes of social control. Primarily, its understanding of offending, despite some challenges (Walker and Beaumont 1981; Jordan and Jones 1988; Arnold and Jordan 1996; Drakeford and Vanstone 1996), has been drawn from psychology. Just as psychological theories have moved in and out of vogue, so too have probation theory and practice, and in the process they have rubbed shoulders with a miscellany of theories about the causes of crime and personal and social problems, including eugenics.

In a challenging account of the rise of the psychology of the individual,

Rose (1996) argues that since the nineteenth century, psychiatry, which he uses as a generic term to cover the work of professionals from psychiatrists to social workers, has engaged with politics and the problems of social control. In his view, controlling the behaviour of others involves experts with a body of knowledge defining the problems to be dealt with and forming a link between governments and the problem-solving 'sites' where behaviour is processed and responded to. So, in the last quarter of the nineteenth and the first quarter of the twentieth centuries psychiatry became pivotal to the application of knowledge to abnormality, and achieved a position of power and influence through its ability to deal with the problems created by dysfunctional behaviour, and *ipso facto* concerns about 'the consequences of hereditary transmission across generations' (p. 61).

Eugenics

Crime was part of that eugenicist concern, and had been throughout the nineteenth century; and likewise the moral philanthropists, in their commitment to reformatory and industrial schools and the penitentiary experiment at Pentonville, demonstrated their categorization of young offenders and other possible future offenders as a distinct group in need of protection from the dangers of moral degeneration (Garland 1985; May 1991b; Taylor 1998). The police court missionaries began their work within this political context, and as what Rose (1985: 174) terms a 'new psychological jurisdiction' emerged to identify the dangerous and the abnormal, their successors, probation officers, joined the 'moral typographers' who in their reports and assessments defined criminality as a contagious disease. Because, therefore, probation has been so closely associated with the psychology of the individual, and because psychology's ambition to be a relevant science was articulated in the vocabulary of degeneracy, its humanitarian tradition must be judged by this more complex interpretation. It is, we argue, central to an understanding of the early history of probation. How, then, can the theory that the early history of probation is embroiled in eugenics, moral degeneracy and psychological aspiration, and that humanitarianism is an inadequate explanation for the development of community supervision of offenders, be demonstrated?

Although the eugenicists were challenged by some, their influence was pervasive: indeed, the vocabulary of eugenics, with its familiar litany of labels – criminals, gamblers, drunks, paupers, imbeciles, idiots, vagrants, the mad and so on – permeates the discourse of the reformers. Later, the mental hygiene movement, which Rose clarifies as a more positive way of looking at the same categories, became a component of psychiatry's 'non-custodial project' centred in, for example, courts and schools, and aimed at reducing the social danger emanating from deviant behaviour of one kind or another (Rose 1996: 10) – but more of that later.

As we stated earlier, Matthew Davenport Hill, a recorder in Birmingham in the mid-nineteenth century who began the practice of releasing juveniles on recognizance, is noted as an influential figure in the history of community sentences (Bartrip 1975), and an examination of his writings illustrates the contradictions in his reformative zeal. Undoubtedly he was a humanitarian, keenly interested in reform; he was a strong advocate of the administration of justice in mercy; and prisons, to him, were places where offenders should be morally and religiously enlightened (Hill 1857). However, like many of his contemporaries, he believed in transportation and lengthy periods of imprisonment for certain categories of prisoner, and he believed that the mental and physical inferiority of criminals in general was easily apparent when seeing large numbers of them. Nor was he in any sense committed to the idea of equality: following the Chartist demonstration of 10 April 1848, he dismissed the idea of equality because of 'the vast inequalities resulting from diversities in the structure and cultivation of the mind, giving to one human being superiority over another to an extent absolutely immeasurable'. It was, he continued, therefore inappropriate for the law to redistribute the wealth of those in society who were skilful, hard-working and careful with their money to 'make up the deficit of the inexpert, the slothful and the prodigal' (Hill 1857: 114). If Hill was influential, the Howard Association was of critical importance to political acceptance of the idea of community supervision through probation (Le Mesurier 1935), and its role requires examination.

The Howard Association

It began its life at a meeting in Stoke Newington (Rose 1961), and its annual reports from 1873 to 1912 demonstrate that its campaign for reform had clear humanitarian motivation – for instance, its pressure for prison reform focused on remunerative prison work that prepared prisoners to earn an honest living outside; it was concerned about mortality rates caused by a combination of low diet and the treadmill (Howard Association 1867, 1868); and it recognized the dire plight of the poor. Some members visited America, studied the American system of probation and prepared influential reports. In August 1881 Joseph Sturge, one of the founders of the reformatory system, visited Massachusetts and examined its Juvenile Probation and State Agency. The report of that year provides a detailed account which argues for the introduction of the system into Britain (Howard Association 1881). The campaign to introduce the Massachusetts model was furthered by the recommendations of a Miss Hughes (Howard Association 1902, 1903), and Miss Lucy Bartlett, a member of the Association's committee, both of whom had spent several months observing the systems in Boston, Chicago, New York and Philadelphia (Howard Association 1905). Thomas Holmes and Edward Grubb (present and past secretaries of the Association) argued for the appointment of probation officers by the Home Office and under the control of the courts in a meeting with Gladstone, the Home Secretary (Howard Association 1906).

However, this campaign was underscored by concerns about moral degeneracy, a clear ideological and political position, and a theoretical understanding of the causes of crime, namely, intemperance, education that is 'perverted when it is so one-sided as to convey a practical contempt for labour', lack of religious and moral training in the right habits, and improvidence (Howard Association 1878: 18). The responsibility for crime, it believed, was therefore firmly that of the individual: although the environment had an impact on people, individuals were to a 'far greater and more general degree' to blame for their situation; and it illustrated its point by referring to neat new cottages in Walthamstow that had been turned into slums by 'a morally low class' of occupants (Howard Association 1884: 4). Subscription to the notions of individual responsibility and state power was always near the surface. It promoted the idea of supportive counselling through probation, but only if backed by the threat of imprisonment in order to prevent lazy and drunken parents foisting their children 'upon the backs of the rate and taxpayers' (Howard Association 1884: 6). Moreover, it argued for changes in the law to allow for the longer detention of vagrants in the labour wards of poor houses; the removal of the evil of unconditional almsgiving; local committees for administrating poor relief; repeal of the law of settlement and removal of paupers; an end to laxity towards hawkers and peddlers (who were deemed vagrants); and separate cells in casual wards (Howard Association 1882: 3–4).

The idiom of eugenics and a connection with the general political anxieties about social degeneracy permeate the reports. It was concerned that reformatories and industrial schools 'might become sources of pauperism and communism', and '[t]he children of the lazy, vicious, the drunkard and the criminal may be thrown, in increasing thousands, upon the shoulder of the honest taxpayer' (Howard Association 1882: 18), and that crowding juveniles and adults into large institutions, either penal or charitable, would increase the 'mischievous tendencies of the promiscuous' (Howard Association 1883: 3). In another report it discussed the habitual offenders of the 'Dissolute Class', and recommended farm colonies and Magdalene institutions with enforced remunerative labour instead of prison plus care for the feeble-minded and half insane (Howard Association 1904). It was selective in who should qualify for community supervision, and excluded the 'dangerous classes', namely defectives, habitual misdemeanants and habitual criminals (Howard Association 1906).

The language of humanitarianism

The contradictory nature of the humanitarianism of the reform movement and its connection with classical criminology and some of the foundations of future eugenic ideology are further underlined by the writings of William Tallack and Thomas Holmes, who were at different times secretary of the Association. In a paper presented to a meeting of American prison officers in New York, Tallack (1871) acknowledges poverty as a significant contributory factor to crime, and underlines the need for thoughtful and discerning use of penal discipline. However, his elaboration of this point reveals his ideological position: poverty, he claims, causes physical and psychological defects which are passed on as 'hereditary misfortunes'; 'in by far the greater proportion of offences, crime is hereditary'; and prisoners, 'as a class, are of mean and defective intellect, generally stupid' (p. 23). Like many of his contemporaries, he believed in the doctrine of less eligibility and that teaching prisoners to read and write made them more dangerous on discharge. This is his attempt to replace 'morbid leniency' and 'unwise humanitarianism' with 'genuine humanity' (an early version of 'tough love'). In another paper (Tallack 1872), he reasserts his belief that in most cases crime is hereditary and associated with some bodily defect (p. 99), but then turns his argument on its head by challenging determinism and defining offenders as morally responsible citizens worthy of the chance to reform.

Garland (1985: 101) is correct when he refers to Thomas Holmes as a 'less explicit eugenist'. Holmes worked for many years as a police court missionary, and displayed his humanity in practical ways, but it was a humanity informed by a curiously hybrid philosophy (Holmes 1908). He was prepared to imprison people in his home for their own good (p. 116), and he thought that some groups of people should be detained indefinitely. On the one hand, he asserts that people 'become criminals not because they possess criminal minds, but because there is no place for them in our social and industrial life; because their necessities cannot be supplied in any other way' (Holmes 1912: 39), and because they cannot compete with the fitter. On the other hand, offenders are 'morally diseased' and 'weakness, not wickedness, is the one general cause of crime' (p. 24). Moreover, he is selective about who deserves his sympathy: he has no time for the 'idle, loafing criminal' but much more for 'the intelligent and industrious criminal' (Holmes 1908: 132). In the same work, he could announce that he does not believe that the 'degenerate' is a criminal, but that he supports the practice in Holland of permanent detention and complete segregation so that there could be no 'opportunities of perpetuating their kind' (Holmes 1912: 81).

Similar convolutions can be discerned in the words of other significant figures in the reform movement which straddled the end of the nineteenth and beginning of the twentieth centuries. Howard Vincent, in promoting his Probation of Offenders Bill, underlined the importance of social order and his lack of sentimentality towards habitual offenders; for him, their crimes were the 'product of a criminal and habitually vicious mind' (Hansard 1886: 333–4). Dr W.A. Potts, a regular contributor to probation conferences and publications, Chairman of the Birmingham After-Care Committee and advocate of community sentences, could describe a young female offender as a 'degenerate' with a 'congenital tendency' and a marked 'moral defect' (Potts 1903: 89). Ruggles-Brise, in his preface to Goring's *The English Convict*, concludes that the offender is 'to a large extent, a "defective" man, either physically or mentally' (Goring 1919: v). Goring himself claimed as 'indisputable fact' that 'on average, the Criminal of English prisons is markedly differentiated by defective physique ... defective mental capacity ... and by an increased possession of anti-social proclivities', and that he and his researchers found 'the criminal to be unquestionably a product of the most prolific stocks in the general community' (p. 272). The Prison Commissioner, Edmund du Cane (1885) insists that the deliberate, rational offender and the 'weak-minded or imbecile' are both incurable, and need to be 'dealt with on different principles from those others who may by appropriate treatment be deterred or reformed' (pp. 4–5). Robert Holmes, another police court missionary and then probation officer, warns society about failing to intervene in dysfunctional families because 'the children will in turn propagate the evil which increases and will increase until a remedy is applied – a remedy involving some sacrifice, but ready to hand' (Holmes 1915: 25).

There is a case for arguing that belief in degeneracy and the need to be selective permeated probation ideology from its inception: for example, John Augustus excluded those who were 'wholly depraved' from his reformatory efforts (John Augustus, quoted in White 1978). Although it is a belief that needs to be placed in its historical and contemporary context, it needs emphasis in order to complete a fuller picture of the humanitarianism that led to community supervision, and to explain how, in the Victorian penal system, criminals were clustered in the lowest stratum of the community, set apart from their 'more respectable peers' and perceived as a constant source of contamination (Garland 1985: 38). This was the result, Garland argues, of an amalgamation of ideologies drawn from criminology, eugenics and religion, and the gift of charity (with its baggage of duty, guilt and social superiority), and it accorded social work the task of maintaining order through reforming the individual. Of these, Christianity had a particularly prominent role in both the dominant ideologies and the provision of this aspect of philanthropy, and merits more than just a passing glance.

Christian charity

The work of the missionaries and the temperance movement had been conceptualized as a crusade from the beginning (*Church of England Temperance Chronicle* 1873), but it was a crusade also embroiled in political conflict. The Chartists doubted whether moral exhortation promoted the interests of poor people, and some socialists believed that the movement sustained intemperance as an effective means of illuminating 'working class vices' (Harrison 1971: 403). By implication those doubts extend more generally to social work, police court missionary work and later to probation because, as Bowpitt (1998) explains, evangelical Christianity was an essential part of each. Eventually, it would diminish in significance because science was eventually to prevail over 'saving souls', and the language of eugenics and determinism referred to above can be interpreted as a part of the drift towards scientific explanation in work with offenders. Bowpitt provides an interesting explanation for this in a reappraisal of the Christian origins of social work and a contrasting of the evolving practice of social work and the revivalism of the evangelicals that characterized Victorian philanthropy.

He highlights the commitment within the social work project to social improvement through social action rather than evangelism or state intervention as the reason for its subsequent break from philanthropy and dependence on rationality and social science. While acknowledging the close connection between charity and its evangelical Methodism, on the one hand, and early social work with its flimsy knowledge base, on the other hand, he then explains the split in terms of the secularization of society at the end of the nineteenth century and the inherent flexibility of liberals within the Church of England in the face of the challenge of science. Further impetus was given to secularization, he argues, first by the philosophical idealism of Oxford intellectuals in the 1870s and 1880s and its notions of the potential of the individual, moral citizenship, self-reliance and civic duty; and second by the Charity Organisation Society, founded as it was on 'moral and social improvement' rather than spiritual redemption. The latter encouraged the 'application of social scientific knowledge to the solution of social problems' (Bowpitt 1998: 683), which in social work took the form of attempts to change the individual and transform pauperism into self-reliance. Interestingly, this complements, rather than contradicts, McWilliams's (1983) theory that the evangelists gave way to the social diagnosticians because of the deterministic implications of helping people to overcome the 'stumbling block' of drink. Bowpitt, along with others (Young 1976; Garland 1985), accords significance to the Charity Organisation Society in the development of professional aspirations in social work through its campaign against indiscriminate almsgiving, and it is here that political and Christian motivations conjoin. While Bowpitt's analysis is valuable for the further insight it gives into the early history of social work, it overestimates the difference between moral improvement and spiritual redemption. The importance of spiritual redemption continued to be emphasized well into the twentieth century, and, in early probation history at least, the two remain prominent objectives of intervention. As late as 1925, a Nottingham probation officer confirmed the spiritual dimension to probation by arguing that while helping people in practical ways, probation officers should never neglect 'the great evangelical principle of the regenerating and sanctifying work of the spirit of God' (Poulton 1925: 546). The pre-eminence of the religious motive and focus on spirituality was continued, at least, for the first half of the twentieth century, and is confirmed by several historians of probation and the mission (Potter 1927; Dark 1939).

Other forms of community sentence

Inevitably, the discussion about the origins of community sentences has focused on the probation order, but the story of both the political and social context has also included a number of different variants of community sentence. These include the voluntary and statutory after-care of prisoners, supervision orders, combination orders and community service.

Work with prisoners began in the early part of the nineteenth century with the activities of a small number of discharged prisoners' aid societies that before 1862 served local county gaols (NADPAS, 1956). The police court missionaries became involved when a prison gate mission was set up in Liverpool in 1879, and on discharge prisoners were offered a free breakfast in the mission and were invited to sign the 'pledge' (Jarvis 1972). The societies continued their involvement well into the twentieth century, but police court missionaries and later probation officers supervised prisoners too; and by 1925 after-care work had extended the supervision of young offenders after their release on behalf of the Home Office schools and the Borstal Association (Bochel, 1976). This situation, in which a number of agencies were involved in dealing with prisoners, continued until the Advisory Council on the Treatment of Offenders (1963) recommended that the probation service assumed primary responsibility for after-care. Increasingly, the responsibilities of the service in this area of work moved from voluntary to statutory supervision through the extension first of parole and subsequently of conditional release following the recommendations of the Carlisle Committee's report on parole in England and Wales (Home Office 1988b).

Community service was introduced in 1973 following the recommendations of the Wootton Report (Home Office 1970); this was a new sentence which did not involve social work supervision, but instead a kind of generalized reparation through the completion of tasks in the community, many of which had a practical orientation. Following a two-year experimental period, and the publication of a somewhat inconclusive report, community service expanded rapidly to become a very significant part of the service's role. Following the Criminal Justice Act 1991, it also became possible for courts to combine the elements of the probation order and community service into one order, namely the combination order.

The point to be made about these excursions into slightly different areas of work is that they too are a part of the political and moral context described above. The supervision of prisoners in its earlier guise may have had a more practical focus, but it was also based on a morally and religiously informed view of what prisoners needed; and in its later statutory form, initially at least, it was as embroiled in the treatment model as mainstream probation. Although, before the advent of the combination order, community service lived its life outside that model, it retained elements of the idea of reformation of the character through good works and self-reflection and it certainly derived from a particular moral and political view of society. So, combination orders and community service orders form part of the range of community sentences or what are called in America 'intermediate sanctions', and they too are best understood against the historical backdrop described above.

Conclusion

In this chapter, we have not set out to reduce the humanitarian tradition of community supervision to a level of insignificance. Indisputably, it was a key driving force in the reform movement, and played an important role in the displacement of prison as a sentence of first resort. Moreover, it is likely that the humanitarians were attracted to psychological as well as environmental explanations of crime because it provided reasons for leniency. We have, therefore, argued that the reform movement and probation practitioners were also influenced by moral and political constructions of the nature of people and social problems, and that this led them into the ideological territory of eugenics and mental hygiene. We have seen that important figures in the development of community supervision, like Hill, Tallack and Holmes, were products of their age and that consequently their humanitarianism was tempered by constructions of human behaviour and nature in vogue at the time. It has, therefore, to be embedded more firmly in the broader social, cultural and political context we have outlined. However, we have not suggested that our analysis is groundbreaking; rather, we have argued that it is a dimension of the history of 'community punishment' that hitherto has been underplayed, and that exploring its complexities, far from giving a pejorative slant to that history, actually illuminates it in a way that helps our understanding of current policies and practices. The period covered witnessed a change from voluntary and charitable action to professionalism, and the rise and fall of treatment and rehabilitation as primary criminal justice goals. In the next chapter we pay attention to the work of practitioners, listen to their stories and draw some conclusions about what they tell us about those changes and the ideologies of the supervision of offenders in the community.

Further reading

Many of the early historical texts such as Grinnell (1941), Dark (1939) and Ayscough (1923, 1929) are rather inaccessible to anyone other than social historians who are prepared to search the archives. So, for the general social and political context of the development of probation, readers can do no better than go to Garland (1985, 1990). For a succinct summary, Newburn (1995) is a useful text.

Notes

1 This is the Common Law practice of releasing a person from court to be of good behaviour.
2 Ayscough offers no more explanation than this, and his use of upper-case letters is repeated here.

chapter three

Good intentions and probation practice

Much of the available history about agencies involved in the community supervision of offenders has focused on policy and legislative developments. Far less attention has been given to the theory and practice of supervision, and as the previous chapter demonstrates, in addition to the social and political context in which they existed, the motivations, attitudes and actions of individual practitioners are crucial to a fuller understanding of the community sentences that were the vehicles for such supervision. This chapter, therefore, presents the main practice paradigms, and attempts to demonstrate that the responses of practitioners to the changing policy contexts and available theories and fashions coalesce around a predominantly moral and psychological model.[1]

'Advise, assist and befriend'

In some senses, it is difficult to categorize this familiar phrase as a paradigm because it might be seen by some as a motif of the probation service that straddles all practice throughout its history. However, we would argue that to the extent that it encapsulates the moral, religious (and implied theoretical) bases of the early practice of supervising offenders in the community it stands as a distinct paradigm. Its aim was to redeem by Christian exhortation, and it can be seen in its earliest form in the work of Augustus referred to in the previous chapter. His work encapsulated its primary aim and was tempered by an understanding that the criminal justice system should eschew revenge and punishment in favour of the reform of offenders (Augustus 1939). His contribution to this was to persuade the courts to bail the individual so that subsequently he could provide sufficient evidence of their improved behaviour to warrant a small fine (Chute 1939). As Glueck (1939) indicates, this involved building a friendship and providing practical help, thereby positively influencing the person's behaviour. Augustus, however, dispensed his favours selectively: he was interested primarily in first offenders who displayed contrition and motivation to change, and who were not beyond redemption. In this sense, therefore, he laid the foundation of a selective approach to community supervision to be enacted in both America and the United Kingdom.

What, then, was this early form of intervention in the sentencing process like? It was selection based on moral judgement and it would permeate practitioners' work in the courts through the nineteenth century and into the twentieth. Augustus's work, predicated as it was on selection, friendship, exhortation, persuasion and confrontation, combined with practical help, did provide a template for future practice; however, as White (1978) cautions us, it was a relatively superficial form of supervision.

This could be said also about the work of the police court missionaries who were the precursors to probation officers. Nelson and Batchelor, the first missionaries, began their work in the Southwark, Lambeth, Bow Street and Mansion House courts in the second half of the 1870s within a Victorian criminal justice system predicated on notions of moral culpability and moral degeneracy manifested mainly in drunkenness, and in which prison was the principal response to crime. Their work was motivated and sustained by religious faith and individual theories about crime, and as the recorded work of Nelson attests, it was superficial. It included 438 home visits; 293 police court visits; 165 visits to cab-stands; the taking of 149 pledges; 117 prison visits; 94 visits to workshops; 34 visits to railway stations; and 20 visits to lodging houses (Page 1992: 9). Moreover, during their first five years Nelson and Batchelor interviewed 16,269 prisoners and took 584 pledges (Ayscough 1923). For 30 years the London Diocesan Branch of the Church of England Temperance Society recorded these activities and presented them in annual reports that show a relatively unchanged pattern up to and beyond the introduction of probation.

Despite its superficial nature, what links this practice to the community supervision of the present day is that it was an attempt to change people. It occurred within a Christian framework, and missionaries had to be

Christian if they were 'to exercise any influence for good over those who come within [their] reach' (Ayscough 1923: 36). This early manifestation of a practice paradigm, then, had a strong religious flavour that would survive well into the twentieth century, but it also contained methods that would survive too. A description of the purpose of a home visit in a Church of England Temperance Society (1901: 22) report provides a clue to some of the primary components of the missionary's methodology: relationship building; religiously tinged persuasion and influence; exhortation to self-control; monitoring; what appears to be a prototype of systems intervention; emotional and physical support; financial help and material assistance to find work:

> [t]o take an interest in the drunkard's family, to encourage him in the difficult way of Total Abstinence amid much temptation; to show an appreciation of a hobby in which he is engaged, are ways by which we impart a strength of will and purpose to which the penitent is probably a stranger. There are, too, visits of inquiry, for the purpose of tracing the friends of the prisoner; visits for the purpose of relief in sickness; and for payment of rent, varied possibly by an excursion to a market for the purpose of buying a stock in trade etc.

The writings of Thomas Holmes (see previous chapter), as well as illustrating that some of the work was more substantial, provide a convenient bridge between the practice of missionaries and the early probation officers. They are important also because they reveal the early influence of psychology, a discipline that was not only to assume an increasing importance in community supervision but would also give shape to the later treatment paradigm. However, some commentators (Todd 1964; Page 1992) have argued that police court missionaries had little contact with theories despite the fact that a review of Holmes's writings reveals at least an acquaintance with contemporary psychological theory. He discusses the problems of the people he encounters in psychological terms; for instance, drunkards have 'diseased minds', delusions and deep-seated troubles (Holmes 1902: 48–9). Indeed, his work is full of a sometimes incongruent mix of psychological and religious allusion, humanitarianism and authoritarianism. At one and the same time he can advocate scientific approaches to treatment and salvation, diversion from custody and locking up inebriate women for life for their own good; and he can be humanitarian on the one hand, and a scourge of the wicked on the other. Thus, alcohol problems could be caused by either mental disease or wickedness, and offending by the psychological damage flowing from or 'idle and shiftless habits'; and recalcitrance demanded treatment in custodial settings for periods long enough to remove 'evil habits' (pp. 76–8). Moreover, he believed in the hereditary nature of crime, that '[s]ome people are born thieves' (p. 133). His is a conflicting and sometimes confused ideology, but it contains a congruity with many of the main elements of contemporary criminological thought, and contains contradictions and compromises that would permeate the practice of community supervision of offenders throughout the twentieth century. In short, it was constructed within a social, moral and political framework.

Another writer, Robert Holmes, who had been a police court missionary and then a probation officer for 17 years provides confirmation of the increasingly pseudo-psychological and eugenic tone of much of the writing about practice within this first paradigm (Holmes 1915, 1923). He believed that most offenders were intellectually, physically and morally below average, and '[m]ore often than not they are the offspring of degenerate parents, and more worthy of pity than blame' (Holmes 1923: 144). Moreover, some categories of offender, such as indecent exposers, should be made 'physically incapable of propagating their species [. . .] and ought not to be suffered to bring into the world children tainted by their vice' (p. 151).

This kind of moral extemporizing in the guise of theory prompted calls for education and training. Gamon (1907) had argued for the appointment of better-educated people, and Leeson (1914: 88) had urged lessons to be learned from the fact that the American system was undermined 'when administered by officers lacking . . . education and training'. Here we see the growing tension between evangelical zeal and professional aspiration. It would be false to locate that tension in the period of transition from police court missionaries to probation officers, but it is evident in early probation discourse. Although, by the time Leeson (1914) and Chinn (1916) were practising as probation officers, the modern complex was well established – with its scientific curiosity, treatment in an increasing number of sites both in and outside the community, and its focus on the psychology of the individual, the assessment and classification of offenders, and the science of eugenics – community supervision still took place largely within a Christian framework.

Some of the writings of the first probation officers provide evidence of this. For example, one probation officer, in an address to the annual conference of rescue workers, argued that the qualities of an officer should include 'deep religious convictions, steadfastness of purpose, with abundance of patience and tact[;] intuition and plenty of sympathy[;] a sense of humour[;] a healthy mind and a healthy body' – as well as 'abundant hopefulness'; 'charity that thinketh no evil'; and 'firmness with open-mindedness' (Pickersgill-Cunliffe 1913: 115). Although she makes no specific reference to theoretical knowledge, she does identify several of the characteristics of the later casework approach, and she exudes a commitment to the notions of moral and mental hygiene. As we argued in Chapter 2, Potter (1927) confirms the legacy of this Christian perspective, and its survival. He asserts that the police court mission was established 'in the overcoming power of the living Christ', and that the spiritual dimension to the work survived well into the take-over by probation (p. 10). For him, this dimension was essential for the trained worker, and the needs of clients were best met by 'the personal contact of a kindly, experienced Christian man or woman' (p. 53).

Gamon (1907), commissioned as he was by the Toynbee Trust to observe the police courts and talk to missionaries, clergy and employers, provides a more objective view. After 12 months of research and observation he concluded that 'the friend in the police-court, par excellence, is the police-court missionary. He is the friend of all alike, and the friend simply, never the prosecutor' (p. 161). However, he qualifies this description with a more critical edge to his judgement about the workers who shortly were to become the first probation officers. According to his account, the missionary was not always welcome in the courts, and although his position was officially recognized, some magistrates were reluctant to consult him, and for much of the time ignored him. His salary, education and qualifications created a lack of status, and put him in a 'wholly subordinate position' to both police and clerks. Moreover, the missionary, although well intentioned, was 'narrowminded, zealous but inclined to preach' (p. 179). Many of them were to become the first officially appointed probation officers.

The arrival on the scene of the first probation officers did not mean their unquestioned acceptance in the courts. The sometimes disdainful attitudes of the magistrates towards missionaries continued after the enactment of the 1907 legislation, and were manifested in a reluctance to use probation officers. The report of the Departmental Committee on the Probation of Offenders Act (Home Office 1909: 3), barely two years after the first probation officer was appointed, reveals wide discrepancies from court to court: of 513 probation orders made in Britain, 388 of them were made in the London Sessions. The religious attitudes of the missionaries survived too. As indicated above, many of the new probation officers were former police court missionaries, and in court they sat alongside their former colleagues who remained missionaries. McWilliams (1985) has argued that their days as savers of souls were numbered, but the language of religious persuasion would remain despite the slow drift towards a more scientific approach. Furthermore, the literature of probation in its early years, which remained a curious mixture of religion and science liberally sprinkled with what McWilliams has termed uninformed 'moral judgement', also alludes to the fear of social degeneracy, and the now established eugenics movement.

The struggle for professional status was to become more transparent, and this is illustrated graphically by Thomas Holmes's book about psychology and crime in which he opens with the confident assertion that he and his contemporary practitioners know as much about the mind 'as scientists or specialists' (Holmes 1912: 4). He then embarks on a rehearsal of many of the theories about crime causation that set the tone for much of the writing about practice that followed in the first decade of the life of the probation service.

Although it is probable that McWilliams (1986: 255) is right in his judgement that it was not until the 1960s that 'psycho-social diagnosis' had 'swept aside many (though not all) of the earlier understandings', a perusal of the writings of probation officers from the beginning of the 1920s reveals that the language of social science was cropping up amidst the idiom of common sense and religious morality. The publication of the National Association of Probation Officers gave probation officers the opportunity to begin the process of building up a literature about the practice of community supervision. It is a useful source for examples of how they described what they did.

Mrs Cary (1913), who worked in the London courts, describes how she 'coddled' many of the 108 women she worked with over a three-year period. In the same year, Carr (1913: 29) provides one of the earliest examples of familiarity with the new scientific language when he argues that because of the 'intricate and tangled nature of moral disease' it is vital that the 'diagnosis should be a correct one' before 'treatment' is started. His description of the process of diagnosis is pseudo-scientific and medical in tone, and is peppered with the language of eugenics. Using an imaginary case, he delineates the stages of diagnosis. Firstly, he advises, search for the type of motivation and judge whether it is good or not. If it is good because, for example, the case's family are hungry, then it can be concluded that there is 'no chronic moral disorder'. On the other hand, if it is bad because of, for example, 'indolence, habit, cowardice or revenge', then the case is much more difficult and necessitates delving deeper into his history, 'wading through effect and cause to an abominable home in childhood; aye, to the moral disease of parents before childhood' (p. 29). Further insight into practice is provided by his reference to contact with a wide assortment of people and organizations, including parish priests, the National Society for the Prevention of Cruelty to Children, the children officer, the relieving officer, school attendance officer and officials from the Civic Guild – the whole gamut of what Rose (1996) terms 'expert authority'.

A paper written two years later further confirms this impression of professional aspiration wrapped in paper with a confused pattern of pseudo-scientific pretension and Christian morality. Palin (1915: 88) recounts a case where the only hope lies in recourse to an institution in which

> their character may be studied, their weakness strengthened, their failings watched and overcome, their besetting sin subdued; where they may become respectable, honest law abiding citizens; where love and duty to their saviour and to their fellow creatures may become a dominant feature of their lives, so that when entering the world again they may be able to stand firm and fight against the temptations of the world, the flesh and the devil.

He depicts the probation officer as a specialist, akin to a physician, who should choose carefully a home appropriate to the young person's needs, and 'pledged in the sight of God', use his knowledge of that young person's home background, his friends and the general environment in which they offended (p. 89).

In the same edition, Crabb (1915) describes the nature of the relationship between officer and probationer, and in so doing neatly encapsulates the combination of help and authority inherent in, at least, the intention of practice. The 'wayward and outcast' is advised and helped,

> not merely to supervise him and restrain him with a law of iron, in fear of pains and penalties for an arbitrary period, but to assist the fallen in remoulding his own character, to be the gardener of the man's soul, to assist in eradicating the weeds of ill, and to nurture and foster the better qualities that are in him (p. 98).

The issue of moral degeneracy is brought into stark relief in a paper on the nature of crime causation and society's response (Helmsley 1915). A litany of causes is delineated which echoes the work of others both inside and outside the service (Ellis 1910; Holmes 1912; Goring 1919): lack of parental control: the excessive drinking of parents; 'the degeneracy or degradation of development from the normal type'; 'defective physique'; 'imperfectly developed intellect' and lack of moral education; an environment of crowded houses and filthy streets; lack of self control; and greed (Helmsley 1915: 100). Environment is highlighted as important only because '[d]egenerates and moral lepers are born in the atmosphere of moral and physical rottenness pervading the slums'; they are 'poor creatures', victims of circumstance and born in 'viciousness, immorality, mental and moral derangement' (p. 101). The same ideological outlook is evident in the words of Cecil Leeson, who had been a probation officer for two years when he wrote the first extensive work on the probation system:

> Delinquency is traceable in the last resort either to social defect, or to physical or mental defect, or to both reacting on each other. The readjustments in the former cases constitute the special work of the probation system. Offenders in the defective class need something more than probation, however, unless that term be understood to cover medical diagnosis and treatment; and juvenile court clinics were set up to supply the deficiency.
>
> (Leeson 1914: 25)

In a later paper, Hemsley (1920) concentrates on the offending of 14–20-year-olds and asserts that boys are less of a problem than girls; that the crimes of adolescents are more likely to be associated with immoral tendencies; and that the major cause of offending is lack of parental control. Then, she captures the mixture of fledgling social science and Christian homily by advising that the 'moral reformer' should match 'his or her Patient's diverse complaints' (p. 221). Indeed, the growing influence of social science is evident in the emergence of the concept of casework in probation officers' discourse. Moreover, while the notion of 'advise, assist and befriend' survived, casework encompassed the next dominant paradigm, treatment.

The treatment model

The conflict between science and religion, emanating as it did from a reform movement that represented the demands of the criminological programme while rejecting 'the basic tenets of criminological science in favour of common-sense and an evangelical conscience' (Garland 1985: 124), dominated the practice and theory of community supervision certainly for the first half of the twentieth century. However, that supervision was an integral part of the process of individualization in the penal system, with its new found curiosity about the individual; and it took its place in a 'system of individual superintendence' designed to achieve an 'awakening of conscience' in that individual (Saleilles 1911). It was tied, therefore, to the psychology, with its 'new rationales and techniques', of 'all those strategies, forms of thought and action, that seek to conduct the conduct of others' (Rose 1996: 3), and in turn led to an inevitable growth in knowledge and administrative structures. In particular, probation followed a path through the fields of eugenics and social degeneracy concern, assuming the mantle of respectability of evangelical humanitarianism, but as efforts to change human behaviour became more demanding, probation officers became increasingly interested in 'the application of psychology, and of what are now recognised as case-work techniques, to the social work of the courts' (Bochel 1976: 121).

Evidence of this progression and an increasing recognition of the complexity of problems associated with offending can be seen in a paper on the 'difficult case' (Rankin 1921), in which the author reflects (as an expert in the criminological branch of sociology) on the causes of crime. He denies having ever met a born criminal, but speculates about causality in terms of inherited wickedness and immorality, social circumstances or 'pathological craving for excitement' (p. 321). Another officer, Membury (1922), displays his method, which begins with diagnosis or the 'probe', a dig into the foundations of the history of not just the subject but also his parents. His interest is in whether the problem is 'Mental, Physical or deliberately Criminal' or a combination of all three; or whether it is of 'pre-natal origin' or 'hereditary', or of 'environment'; or whether it is the consequence of 'the fruit of kindness or of gross carelessness' (p. 345).

Running parallel to such thinking were growing demands for more training and education. A magistrate, after visiting America, argued for probation to be placed on a par with teaching, and training, 'on and off the job', and a 'technique based on scientific principles'; he called for a national probation service with 'conditions of service, pay and pension adequate to a high calling' (Trought 1925: 510). Chinn (1926), according to Bochel the first officer to use the term 'casework', by implication endorses Trought's argument when, in an exploration of the problem of adolescent sexuality, he refers to the work of three prominent psychologists: Stanley Hall's *Adolescence*, McDougal's *Social Psychology* and William White's *The Mental Hygiene of Children*.

The foundations of casework were laid during the 1920s and 1930s, then, by people like Chinn and Dr W.A. Potts of Birmingham, a significant and clearly influential figure in the probation history of this period. In an address to a branch of the National Association of Probation Officers in the Midlands, Potts (1928) put forward the study of the psychological side of problems as a potential aid to officers. This is an example of the increasing tendency at this stage for groups of probation officers to be exposed to the perceptions and teaching of psychology, and to have expert confirmation of the efficacy of aspects of their practice and the validity of some of their beliefs. As the 1930s dawned, it was a tendency set to increase very significantly.

It is important to recognize, however, that the psychological complex itself was made up of competing influences. The eugenicists, as Rose (1996) has indicated, while opposed by civil libertarians and the mental hygiene movement, had created fertile ground for psychologists by giving prominence to a large group of people classified as degenerate. Nevertheless, the mental hygiene movement had become an integral part of the 'non-custodial project' being enacted in the courts. In so far as offending had become part of the general problem of mental hygiene, probation was drawn into the processes of psychological assessment and classification.

The tensions between these two aspects of the psychology of the individual can be seen both in the language of the papers and addresses by psychologists that began to appear in probation literature, and in the fact that the problems of poverty, social psychology and the psychology of crime featured in the 1930 Home Office National Training Scheme (Le Mesurier 1935: 66). So, for example, in the opinion of one member of the Tavistock clinic, 'normal' delinquency is caused by 'self-indulgence and recklessness, indiscipline, thoughtlessness, conceit' (Suttie 1930), but for another offending is linked to 'taint of mental defect or some racial poison in the family' (Burns 1930: 52). The former sees the probation officer's task as helping the process of growing up, and the latter argues that the probation officer must use his personality 'to free probationers from problems that have twisted essential goodness' (Burns 1930: 52). Both views exemplify the tension between eugenicist and mental hygiene analysis, but it was the latter perspective that was to hold sway – it did, after all, provide more fertile ground for the application of psychological theories and techniques, and more optimism about the possibilities of change (Rose 1996): delinquency was becoming 'a part of the general problem of Mental Hygiene' (Le Mesurier 1935: 208). However, the idea of hereditary defect refused to die: for example, Mrs C.B.S. Hodson, the General Secretary of the Eugenics Society from 1920 to 1931, and a pre-war supporter of the National Socialists in Germany, was given a voice in the probation journal in 1932 (Hodson 1932).

What these contributions serve to exemplify is the increasingly dominant position of psychology in the ideology of those experts who were influencing the service, despite continued exhortation to probation officers to explore the link between faith and science (Talbot 1934), and warnings about the dangers of the weakening influence of religion (Lord Bishop of Chichester 1932),[2] and Talbot (1934). The manifestation of this influence in general social work as well as probation was an American-style casework or 'intelligent and constructive casework', and 'intelligently directed individual treatment' (Chinn 1930: 58–9). In home visiting this meant in-depth study of the family; a focus on maladjustment; planned treatment; sympathy conveyed through a balanced approach as an official and a friend; methodical fact-finding unbiased, objective and free from prejudice; and note-taking (Chinn 1931: 84). Another probation officer introduces the idea of adaptability through modifiable treatment plans (Francis 1932), and Mayling (1933) employs Burt's *The Young Delinquent* to emphasize the need for a comprehensive knowledge base for treatment. Other contributions to the probation journal at this time confirm that casework also remained embedded in moral judgement, Christian mores and class perspectives. Thus, the problems of unemployment and insecurity are products of individual failings of money management and wastefulness that do not occur 'in another class' (Goldstone 1932: 186); and the decline in standards of morality and discipline are encouraged by psychologists and their protestations against the repression of the child (Way 1932). In fact, these chronicles of practice and ideology include most of the ingredients of an approach to the community supervision of offenders that were to prevail for at least the next 40 years. Moreover, each in its own way illustrates the aspiration to professional status, although it was the publication of the *Handbook of Probation* (Le Mesurier 1935) that drew the different strands of this aspiration together to form the first coherent set of guidelines for probation officers. Although it defines probation as a vocation and gives religion a place in successful work, it highlights public protection, the importance of the relationship between client and officer and the need for training, particularly in psychology (pp. 61–2).

The origins of casework have been traced to the work of the Family Casework Agency[3] set up by the Charity Organisation Society (Paskell 1954), but the consolidation of the approach in probation work (at least, as an ideal) began in the 1930s and permeated practitioner discourse in the journal *Probation* in the 1940s. The practitioners' version was influenced heavily by the medical model and a combination of the prevailing theories and homespun philosophy. The new 'scientific approach' embraced all kinds of explanations for offending: mothers and their 'trivial carelessness' and 'lack of elementary routine' (Kennedy 1941: 225); the absence of male teachers through active service 'and the consequent increase of feminine influence over boys already deprived of male personal control' (Gwym 1941: 227); too much free expression in education (Percival 1941). By the beginning of the 1950s confidence in the capacity of the psycho-dynamic model, on which probation practice was purportedly based, to reduce people's offending was high:

> [t]he probation officer finds his inspiration in the sure knowledge that he is the agent of a penal treatment which is both positive and constructive, a treatment which seeks in a difficult section of the community to cherish human rights, integrity and essential goodness.
>
> (Paskell 1954: 92)

Probation practice was indeed both an art and a science (Fry 1954), and community supervision had become 'the application of modern scientific case work to individuals outside institutions' (Younghusband 1954: 123).

Although there was an absence of any evidence from research findings, probation and its accompanying theories, such as maturation theory, were proclaimed as an effective form of treatment (Newton 1956; Raeburn 1958; Dawtry 1958). Officers continued to pursue the professionalism that the expertise of casework was deemed to bring, and the casework model was to survive largely unchallenged for another 20 years. Indeed, according to the Morison Committee (Home Office 1962), casework was the emblem of the Service's professional status; and the government of the day promoted the training of probation officers to fulfil their professional work (Fletcher-Cooke 1962). However, the beginning of some doubt about the basis of this confidence can be discerned in the publication of pessimistic findings on the effect of probation by Wilkins (1958). He found 'no significant differences in the outcome of treatments in terms of further convictions': in short, probation was doing no better (nor worse) than custodial sentences (p. 207). This marked the start of a process that was to lead to the next significant paradigm, based as it was on the notion of 'non-treatment'.

The non-treatment paradigm

One of the earliest attacks on the treatment paradigm in its guise as casework came from Wootton (1959) who, in citing psychoanalysis as the means by which social workers acquired their much needed badge of professionalism, refers to a report that the 1919 National Conference of Social Work in the United States was dominated by psychiatry. She also underlines the influence of psychiatry in the United Kingdom:

In this country, if the social workers' surrender to Freud has been less unquestioning than has that of their American colleagues, the influence of psychiatry has certainly been sufficient to revolutionize both the language these workers use and the conception of their role which they present alike to themselves and to others. (p. 270)

Moreover, in her view, what had been accepted generally with 'uncritical admiration' served merely to put up 'a fantastically pretentious façade'. In particular, she asserts,

[m]odern definitions of 'social casework', if taken at their face value, involve claims to powers which verge upon omniscience and omnipotence: one can only suppose that those who perpetuate these claims in cold print must, for some as yet unexplained reason, have been totally deserted by their sense of humour. (p. 271)

Bean (1976) falls short of suggesting, as Wootton does, that the best chance a social worker has of achieving the aims set out by some of the gurus of casework is to marry her client! However, he does continue a critical assault on the treatment model that was to lead to the fragmentation, rather than disintegration, of the treatment model and the demise of casework as the core of probation practice. Instead, it was to reappear in a slightly different guise based on collaboration with the client as more of an equal partner in the transaction, with more choice and expertise. Bean argues that the *social pathology* model is flawed, firstly because it ignores the wider social context; second, because its target, social disease, is not tangible like physical disease; and lastly, because it has a covert moral agenda. Moreover, he questions its role in the growth of humanitarianism, claiming that this was part of a general reformist trend, and that the 'psycho-social manipulations' of the experts had little relationship to that humanitarianism.

According to his analysis, psychoanalysis provided a theoretical framework for diagnosis which did not have to be restricted to medical experts, and from which probation officers could draw their expertise. Fortunately, perhaps, theories such as this, based on 'unconscious mechanisms', were immune to rigorous analysis and fitted the traditional faith-grounded efforts of officers. Moreover, in Bean's opinion, the model had failed to demonstrate its efficacy – not because of a shortage of expertise but because of the fundamental failure of its theoretical perspective on crime in all that perspective's various guises. It was, to use (as he does) Matza's (1964) phrase, 'a system of rampant discretions'. His is a powerful argument against the discretionary power of experts, and Bean urges a reduction in the largely uninformed power of experts, a problem that was later to be addressed by the effective-practice agenda of the late 1990s. That power, expressed as it was in a considerable degree of autonomy, is confirmed by Folkard *et al.* (1966) in their survey of probation work which demonstrates that most officers explained delinquent behaviour by reference to both the individual and the environment, and attempted to influence behaviour through a diverse range of devices: the 'relationship' and individual treatment; material and psychological help and control; and work on the social environment. Their research showed that probation supervision was characterized primarily by low support and low control, and that the main determinant of type of treatment was the officer providing it.

So, May (1991b) correctly asserts that, despite an apparent decline in professional optimism after the 1960s, officers continued attempts at rehabilitation, and he reiterates Bean's scepticism about the humanitarian tradition of the service, sitting uneasily as it did with the detachment and objectivity 'behind which the professional hides and the client suffers' (p. 270). Indeed, there may have been an overestimation of the infiltration of the treatment model into practice. Cooper (1987) argues that officers were loath to accept the decline of the treatment ideal and the traditional values underpinning it, and continued to use the language of the model while practising a more practical version of help. This fits with evidence of a shift away from the treatment model that may have prefigured the non-treatment paradigm of Bottoms and McWilliams (A. Willis 1983).

It may indeed have been an elaborate pretence. The detail of Radzinowicz's (1958) analysis of the effectiveness of probation had exposed the frailty of the impact of probation some years earlier. His 'remarkably favourable response to treatment' (successful completion rates of 79 per cent for adults and 73 per cent for juveniles) may have been sustained for three years, but it was based on work with what now would be termed low-risk offenders. More tellingly, his survey showed that the more convictions probationers had the more rates of success fell. The potency of effectiveness lessened with more recidivistic offenders (51.5 per cent for adults and 42.1 per cent for juveniles).[4] Some 16 years after this study, the IMPACT experiment (Folkard *et al.* 1974, 1976) added further doubt about the efficacy of treatment, although it did suggest that it depended on the matching of treatment to particular categories of offender. In retrospect, its finding that offenders with low criminal tendencies and high levels of problems responded more positively to supervision heralded what would later become a premise of effective practice.[5]

If, then, on the rare occasions that they were empirically tested, casework and the treatment model were found wanting, why were the psychological theories on which they were premised dominant in (at least) the discourse of community supervision? Waterhouse (1983) links their popularity to the fact that they elaborated an explanation of offending that helped officers reconcile the conflict between control and treatment. If the reasons for a person's offending were locked in the unconscious, and predicated on problems with authority or deprivation in childhood, the imposition of expertly defined solutions within a framework of external control could be deemed positive and helpful (Hunt 1964; Foren and Bailey 1968). Of course, it could have been simply because they were promulgated in training.

It was in response to the negative research findings and philosophical misgivings about such reasoning that a number of commentators in the late 1970s and early 1980s (for instance, Bottoms and McWilliams 1979; and Raynor 1985) suggested a more collaborative model with the dual objectives of helping probationers to address their offending and resolve their problems, and positively influencing the criminal justice system itself. Others provided a socialist critique of the criminal justice system (Walker and Beaumont 1981), and although they can be criticized for making assertions based on little empirical evidence and overdependence on one officer and one unpublished survey,[6] they did raise awareness of oppression of black women and men, other women and the poor by criminal justice processes. But, as Raynor *et al.* (1994: 7) have argued, '[t]he practical strategies advocated by political radicals (for example, Hugman, 1980) actually differed little from those which made sense within the "non-treatment" approach', but both shared a 'reliance on ethical or ideological arguments in the absence, to begin with, of really convincing empirical demonstrations that practice based on these models would prove more effective'.

The increasingly evident unease among practitioners and commentators was given a voice in the paper by Bottoms and McWilliams (1979) on the 'non-treatment paradigm'. The confidence of the 1950s and 1960s referred to above had been replaced by doubts about the effectiveness of probation, and the view that offending was some kind of symptom of illness had been discredited not just in criminological discourse but also by research evidence that the 'cure' did not work (Lipton *et al.* 1975; Folkard *et al.* 1976). Although prominent in probation thinking in the past, the Bottoms and McWilliams paradigm perhaps needs explaining to new audiences. It is based on the judgement that the treatment model was theoretically flawed because it contributed to injustice through coerced treatment; it ignored the fact that people choose to commit crime but do not choose to have a disease, and that crime has social causes. Their new framework incorporated four aims: the provision of appropriate help for offenders; the statutory supervision of offenders; the diversion of appropriate offenders from custody; and the reduction of crime. Their central argument was that the notion of *treatment* of crime should be replaced by that of help with client-defined problems. So, treatment becomes help, diagnosis becomes assessment undertaken by worker and client together, and the client's dependent need as the basis for social work action becomes the collaboratively defined task as the basis for social work action. It usefully redrew the framework of probation practice in so far as it identified the offender as an expert resource to be utilized in the change effort. Raynor and Vanstone (1994a) have argued that because it was written at a time of scepticism about effectiveness in reducing offending and before left realist revisionism, and because the authors' 'acceptance that "nothing works" confined them to consideration of crime prevention strategies which had a social focus, to the exclusion of any concern with influencing individuals' (p. 398), the paradigm needs revision 'in a way which preserves its central contribution to improving probation practice' (p. 399). Their revision attempts to retain the core value of 'respect for persons': so help becomes 'help consistent with a commitment to the reduction of harm'; '[s]hared assessment becomes [e]xplicit dialogue and negotiation offering opportunities for informed consent to involvement in a process of change; and [c]ollaboratively defined task becomes [c]ollaboratively defined task relevant to criminogenic needs, and potentially effective in meeting them' (p. 402).

The break with the treatment model has not been total, and in the practitioner literature of the 1980s and 1990s there are numerous examples of work based on a reformulated treatment model predicated on increased collaboration with the offender, the use of contracts and a transparent attempt to link a specific theory or theories to practice. The most recent of these, in effect, reinstates rehabilitation as a central goal of community supervision; it can be described, therefore, as 'new rehabilitation'.

The new rehabilitation paradigm

A significant amount of the work that comes within this paradigm involved working with offenders in groups, so it might be helpful in understanding that work to describe briefly the history of the use of groups in probation supervision. Although the supervision of offenders has largely been undertaken through the use of the one-to-one relationship, the normative potential of groups has been long recognized by probation officers. Miss Croker-King (1915) ran a 'social reporting centre' for 'unclubbables' during the First World War (Page 1992); and another officer set up a social club for girls in hired rooms at a local church institute in Chelsea (Cary 1915). In 1947 Basil Henriques, a London magistrate, established the Highdown Camp for boys from London's East End to encourage 'natural' relationships between probationers and officers (Page 1992). By 1948 trainee probation officers were being taught social psychology, and a component of the course at the University of London's diploma course was 'Recent advances in the study of groups'. In the 1950s evidence emerged of officers working therapeutically with groups. One of the earliest examples involved two probation liaison officers participating in the therapeutic community in the Social Rehabilitation Unit at Belmont Hospital (Parker and Bilston 1959). Another officer worked with 14–15-year-old boys in 'a small experimental therapeutic group' (Bilston 1961). Another had less ambitious aspirations in a discussion group with a small group of adolescents (Ashley 1962). But some tried to apply the theory of casework to groups, for example with a group of seven to nine girls in a hostel (McCullough 1962).

But it was still a minority interest, and when Barr (1966) undertook his survey only 31 probation services out of 125 indicated that they were undertaking some form of groupwork. Although such activity was relatively rare, the observer of one service's work felt able to claim that '[t]he group is, in fact, a very potent medium of social and psychological treatment, in its own right' (Jones 1962: 59). His encouragement seems to have worked, because some 24 years later, Brown and Caddick (1993) discovered 1500 programmes and expressed the view that 'the probation service is the agency most actively involved in the practice of groupwork in Britain today' (p. 16).

Probably the most intensive and concentrated experience of groupwork involving probation officers and other support staff was ushered in with the introduction of the day training centre experiment in 1973. It was to have a strange history in experimental terms (Vanstone and Raynor 1981), and a prominent position in the story of alternatives to prison (Burney 1980; Wright 1984; Vanstone 1985, 1993; Pointing 1986; Mair 1988; Vass 1990; Vass and Weston 1990). But for the purposes of this study, the regimes of the day training centres and subsequent day centres are more important. Outside custodial and residential institutions, they represent the most detailed and structured use of the group as an instrument for rehabilitation in probation's history.

Perhaps the most significant influence on groupwork with offenders in the last 20 years of the twentieth century has been the work of Priestley and McGuire, first through their social skills and personal problem solving approach, and second, through their offending behaviour model (Priestley *et al.* 1978; McGuire and Priestly 1985). Social skills and personal problem solving were the focus of a project funded by the Home Office which ran from 1975 to 1978 in Ashwell and Ranby prisons and the Sheffield Day Training Centre. Drawn mainly from life skills work previously undertaken in Canada (Saskatchewan Newstart 1969), it incorporated cognitive-behavioural methods within a framework of assessment, objective setting, learning and evaluation (Priestley *et al.* 1978, 1984). Following a generally positive evaluation, Priestley and McGuire embarked upon a series of short courses based on the work, and thereby stimulated group programmes for offenders (within the probation service and other relevant agencies) on subjects such as employment, alcohol and drug dependence and rights (see, for example, Singer 1991). Its influence was felt in one-to-one work as well as groupwork (Brown and Seymour 1984).

The offending behaviour model filled a gap in the social skills model by concentrating on the offence. It was implemented initially in the Junction Youth Project in Lambeth, and as if responding to the critiques by Palmer (1975) and Blackburn (1980) of the 'nothing works' message, it soon pervaded practice throughout the United Kingdom; moreover, the groups now focused on offending itself. Although the empirical case for social skills and offending behaviour is not a strong one (Hudson 1988), it has been argued that through their influence on practice (as opposed to policy) both were in the forefront of the 'What Works' project in Britain and contributed to the shift towards evidence-based practice (Vanstone 2000). In retrospect, much of the material for these groups was drawn from cognitive-behavioural work in psychology, and it was to be that theoretical model which would dominate the resurgence of rehabilitation as a goal in the community supervision of offenders. Indeed, the Home Office (1998) championed the principles underpinning the model, and two surveys of effective practice sanctioned by the Home Office (Hedderman and Sugg 1997; Underdown 1998) confirm their pre-eminence in the groupwork of the 1990s.

The story behind the rise of cognitive-behavioural work has been detailed fully elsewhere (McGuire 1995; Raynor and Vanstone 1997; Vanstone 2000) so a summary will suffice. It emerged firstly in the work of Ross and his colleagues in Canada (Ross and Fabiano 1985; Ross *et al.* 1986, 1988), and then in the Straight Thinking On Probation (STOP) programme in Britain, which itself was heavily influenced by that work. Both were a very significant influence on policy and practice in Britain in the 1990s. The series of What Works conferences in the 1990s is clear evidence of that influence (Rowson and McGuire 1992). Ross's original study was a precursor to a number of other research studies and meta-analyses demonstrating effective work with offenders and its characteristics (Andrews *et al.* 1990; McIvor 1990; MacDonald 1993; Trotter 1993; Lipsey 1995), and one that delineated the features of ineffective work (McLaren 1992).

By the end of the twentieth century, then, there was an abundance of cognitive-behavioural work being undertaken in Britain. The most fully evaluated of these, and identified by Underdown (1998) as a properly evaluated programme, is the STOP programme, which was modelled on the Reasoning and Rehabilitation programme developed by Robert Ross and his colleagues in Canada, and established in Mid Glamorgan Probation Service in 1990. What distinguishes the STOP programme, however, is that it was based on a well-researched and validated programme (Ross *et al.* 1985) and required training which was aimed specifically at preparing the officers to deliver the programme so that it met the requirements of programme integrity, namely that the programme was delivered as prescribed.

While for some the STOP programme symbolized a welcome shift to a more informed kind of practice, for others it represented a major fault line in new rehabilitation, paying insufficient attention to the environmental context of people's lives. In other words, it reaffirmed the focus on the individual and the neglect of wider problems. This is an oversimplification, but nevertheless it does draw attention to the fact that during the history of community sentences the wider context has been a peripheral concern. The final paradigm in this chapter, therefore, is one with which a more limited number of managers and practitioners have been concerned.

Beyond offending behaviour

One of its clearest manifestations has been a concern with the impact of discrimination. Raynor *et al.* (1994) argue that there is a need for real concern about oppression and discrimination within the criminal justice system, despite reassurance from some commentators (Harris, 1992). There is a history of disadvantage in the story of black people (Fryer, 1984), and although the evidence for discrimination in the criminal justice system is equivocal it is likely to have impact for some people at each stage of the processing of offenders – from arrest to sentence (Whitehouse, 1983; C. Willis, 1983; Mair, 1986; Hood 1992).

The need for enhancing awareness about racism among probation officers was highlighted at the beginning of the early 1980s in a survey of 30 probation officers (29 white and one of African-Caribbean origin) in an urban centre with a high population of people of African-Caribbean origin (Denney and Carrington 1981). The researchers found that 'probation officers lack an adequate understanding of Rastafarianism' (p. 116), seeing it either as a form of deviance resulting from poor socialization or as a solution to an identity crisis in a hostile environment. Since then anti-discriminatory and anti-oppressive practice has been given a much higher profile within agencies dealing with offenders, and there have been some exemplars of policy and practice. For instance, the Black Offender Initiative (Jenkins and Lawrence 1992), based on a survey of the needs and experience of probation of black probationers, provides an interesting example of work that attempts to counter the effects of discrimination. Another is the Women Offender's Outreach Project (WOOPS), established by Nottinghamshire Probation Service in 1993, which attempts to restructure the use of resources to respond to the particular problems faced by women. It provides guidance and counselling on employment issues, paying particular attention to the problem faced by women who are in a process of change from working in the home to further training, education and employment. Denney (1992) uses a hypothetical team to demonstrate how probation teams can deal with the structural aspects of racism, and the structural dimension to problems of unemployment faced by black people. The team designs a project to focus on these issues in order 'to explore jointly the ramifications and manifestations of racism in this crucial area of everyday life and may connect with the developments of strategies for finding work' (p. 153). But he points to an actual example to reinforce his point – the Handsworth Alternative Scheme, a probation-linked project, which specifically liaises with training and employment projects run by black people.

Discrimination, though, has many facets and permeates the lives of disadvantaged people in several ways (Agozino 1997). It has been argued, for instance, that women and black male and female offenders experience the double jeopardy of unemployment coupled with gender and race, and that therefore social workers, including probation officers, should routinely raise the issue of training and career opportunities with women, provide advice and information, establish self-help groups,[7] form networks with women's employment projects, campaign, and link female probation clients with feminist networks. While the link between poverty and crime is contentious, poverty does underpin the problems of marginalized groups and a significant proportion of people on community sentences (Stewart *et al.* 1989). If we accept McWilliams and Pease's (1990) definition of the help provided by the probation service as 'a moral good expressed by the probation service on behalf of the community', then it is reasonable to argue that the service has a moral responsibility to concern itself with issues of disadvantage and injustice; and when probationers are asked why they offend, poverty is usually near the top of the list. So, how far have probation officers fulfilled this responsibility?

Awareness of the indigence of probationers permeates work from Thomas Holmes through to radical critiques, but the response to it has usually been individualistic. In a description of an early example of a more strategic approach, Ward (1979) reports on discussions in Leeds in 1977 about the need for officers to have greater awareness and knowledge of the fuel debts and welfare rights of probationers living on a large council estate. These led to a steering group being set up with the result that a fuel debts worker was appointed through the Special Temporary Employment Programme and funded by the Manpower Services Commission. The worker analysed all fuel debt cases; networked and generated knowledge within the service about fuel debt issues and Fuel Board policies; set individual problems in a broader context; and promoted the need for advocacy skills among officers.

Likewise, the Social Issues Project was set up in 1988 to improve the skills and knowledge of probation staff in the field of social security and welfare benefits in an attempt to positively change probation practice and policy (Broadbent 1989). It suggested that officers should increase and update their knowledge about relevant legislation; join together with appropriate agencies such as the Child Poverty Action Group and the Low Pay Unit; record and disseminate information that might help problem-solving; set up an advice/help list for probationers; and finally, encourage and support self-help. In another example, the Northumbria Probation Service, in a response to major riots on a housing estate, adopted an anti-poverty policy, appointed a specialist debts and benefits adviser and set up a reporting centre on the estate (Northumbria Probation Service 1994). This was a serious attempt to restructure the provision of services to alleviate the poverty experienced by the people with whom it had contact, and, as Drakeford and Vanstone

(1996) have argued, it provides evidence that some probation services, at least, had learned lessons from the civil disturbances of the 1980s.

Unemployment is closely related to poverty, and Broad (1991) exposes the limitations of one team's approach to the problem in so far as it failed to deal with the problem as a social issue, and present its work 'within a broader social justice framework' (p. 114). However, more recently two probation services, Inner London and Surrey, have established programmes of three years' duration with the specific aim of improving offenders' employment chances (Sarno *et al*. 1999). ASSET, the scheme in Lambeth and Southwark, concentrates on 16–25-year-old black people and offers a range of support and services designed to help them into jobs. The other programme, Surrey Springboard, focuses on offenders under supervision in an attempt to reduce offending 'by providing employment, training and leisure opportunities' (p. 2). Each scheme has been subject to evaluation by Home Office researchers who were interested in how the projects developed and what impact they had. As far as reconviction is concerned, the researchers conclude that the results are 'promising' (45 per cent within one year of first contact in both schemes for 16–25-year-olds), but that controlled comparison is needed before 'firmer conclusions' can be drawn. The response of the offenders was positive, most of the people involved in ASSET, for instance, being 'extremely' positive. Interestingly, the researchers conclude that '[t]he importance of following "what works" principles in running employment programmes cannot be overstated' (p. 1).

Conclusion

In this chapter we have described the main practice paradigms in community supervision. Moreover, we have seen that throughout its history, the practice of supervising people on community sentences has been driven largely by attempts to change individual behaviour rather than the social environment in which that has been played out. The examination of the story of practice rather than policy has thrown a different light on the canvas of that history, and to a significant extent confirmed the arguments of the previous chapter. By and large, practitioners sought their sense of professional identity in the ideology of social casework and the pseudo-medical baggage that came with it, and until the final quarter of the twentieth century functioned in a relatively uncritical socio-political environment. The demise of faith in treatment appeared to have little effect on attempts by practitioners to rehabilitate those under their supervision, but as the century came to an end it did lead to a concerted effort to redefine that activity within a framework of evaluation and accountability. In the next chapter we explore that process in much more detail.

Further reading

The best introduction to the history and development of probation can be found in McWilliams's quartet of papers published in the *Howard Journal of Criminal Justice* (McWilliams 1983, 1985, 1986, 1987). Probably the fullest account of the administrative and legislative history of probation is Bochel (1976). However, any reader serious about exploring the wider sociological dimensions to that history should go to Young (1976). A full revisionist history is contained in Vanstone (2001).

Notes

1 Like the revised history in the previous chapter, this is based on original research by one of the authors.
2 In an address to the July 1932 conference of the National Association of Probation Officers the Lord Bishop of Chichester warned of the dangers of the weakening influence of religion in relation to crime in the face of the growing impact of psychology (see *Probation,* 1(12), 1932). Conference Address, 181.
3 Paskell's use of the word 'Casework' in the title of the agency needs to be viewed with some caution as it seems unlikely that the word would have been in common usage at the time the Charity Organisation Society was established.
4 The conclusions drawn from this research should be viewed cautiously because of the lack of an adequate comparison group.
5 See Chapter 4 for a more detailed discussion of research into probation effectiveness.
6 An officer by the name of Parkinson who several years earlier was steeped in his own version of psychoanalysis; and a Nottingham Probation Service survey.
7 See Jones *et al.* (1993) for an interesting probation example.

chapter four

Does anything work? The emergence of an empirical critique

As we have tried to show in the previous two chapters, to understand the current position of community sentences we need to appreciate the contribution and effects of a long history of practice, itself always located within the social assumptions and received criminological ideas of its time. The same is true of one of the central controversies which has shaped the role and perception of all attempts to supervise offenders in the community: are such attempts effective in reducing offending? Or, to put the question in the simplified form which has tended to dominate too much of the debate, does anything work? In this chapter, as a background to and context for our later account of contemporary developments, we review the history of research on the effectiveness of probation up to the end of the 1980s to show how it affected (and whether it affected) the way the role and purposes of community penalties were (and are still being) understood. We do not aim to cover every study, but to concentrate on those which appeared to have an influence on policy or practice, and in a few cases those which should have had an influence but did not. More recent research – in particular, research which has influenced and supported the 'What Works' movement of the 1990s – will be discussed in Chapter 6.

Although some researchers would clearly like it to do so, research does not seem to influence policy or practice in a direct and simple way. Research which fits, augments or provides a rationale for the policy climate of the time will often achieve a degree of prominence and influence for that reason, while research of comparable or sometimes greater merit and rigour which does not fit in the same way will attract less attention; sometimes it comes into its own when the climate changes, or sometimes it is doomed to become part of a marginal critique outside the mainstream of thinking. Much research funding, particularly government funding of criminal justice research, concentrates on finding answers to questions identified as important by policy-makers, which are often to do with effective implementation of a policy line which has already been decided rather than asking whether the policy itself is fundamentally misconceived. Findings which are not clear-cut and lend themselves to a number of interpretations are likely to receive the interpretation which fits the culture of the times: studies once interpreted as evidence that 'nothing worked' are reinterpreted as evidence that 'some things do work', reflecting what their readers are looking for when they read.

This chapter aims to explore some of the interactions between policy and practice development and evaluative research in probation. As already emphasized, over the years there have been major shifts in both official and professional thinking about the role and function of probation services and about the purposes and aims of probation orders; these have both influenced and been influenced by evaluative research, though never determined by it, and the questions asked by researchers have both reflected and helped to shape the ideas behind official policy. Researchers cannot evaluate a process or activity unless they have some idea of its purposes, and they cannot simply invent these for themselves or the results of their evaluations will be of little use; conversely, purposes formed by policy-makers or practitioners need to be informed by ideas about what is in practice feasible or achievable. As moral philosophers put it, 'ought implies can'. It has also been argued that activities with such a long professional and institutional history as probation come to have their own inherent purposes, and that the aims of a social practice become, in effect, part of its definition, not something which can be altered at will by shifts in policy: its purposes and values are expressed by the activity itself and should inform both evaluation and policy development (McWilliams 1990).

This argument has some force, mainly as an indication of limits: although this book describes considerable changes in probation services and the delivery of community sentences, it is possible to imagine even greater changes of such a scale and scope that to retain the same names would become misleading or unhelpful. Such a change of name was actually proposed for probation in England and Wales by the government in 1999, precisely in an attempt to create an impression of radical change in role and focus: the probation service was to become the Community Punishment and Rehabilitation Service.

The failure of this proposal to attract much support outside government political circles can be taken as a sign that most people still see, or wish to see, a continuity of purpose and function underlying these changes. (Instead the name became, on 1 April 2001, the National Probation Service for England and Wales.) This chapter concentrates on the changes rather than the continuity, but they are changes within a continuing social institution and a largely continuing set of practices.

As we have already seen, the history of probation in England and Wales goes back more than a hundred years, but this chapter is mainly concerned with the last quarter of this history. Even within the relatively brief period of the last 25 years it is possible to identify at least two and possibly three major transformations in official and professional thinking about probation, each of which has had different effects on the issues investigated by probation researchers and on the nature of the dialogue between research, policy and practice. In addition, the picture has been complicated by other factors such as the location of research inside and outside government departments, and by political changes which have been particularly marked during the 1990s. The particular focus of this chapter is on the relationship between the changing evidence base and the changing policy agenda (especially in the 1970s and 1980s), and how they have influenced each other. The selection of particular research studies for comment does not mean that there have not been others, or that others are unimportant; however, we have tried to select those which reflect most clearly the way in which the concept of probation has changed during this period.

Rethinking probation at least twice

What, then, have been the major changes in thinking? Early British studies of the effects of probation, such as Wilkins (1958), and Radzinowicz (1958) were clearly located within what subsequently became known as the 'treatment model': in Radzinowicz's formulation, probation was 'a form of social service preventing further crime by a readjustment of the culprit', and studies were designed to measure whether this readjustment had been successfully achieved. They investigated reconviction, assumed to be a surrogate measure of reoffending. The Home Office Research Unit (as it was then known) undertook a number of ambitious studies of probation and related areas during the late 1960s and early 1970s, including some very complex and sophisticated investigations such as Davies (1974), in a determined search for the effects of probation on recidivism: some of these studies will be further discussed later in the chapter. For the moment, it is sufficient to note that they were concerned with the effects of probation on offenders' behaviour, and took it for granted that this was what probation was about. The professional literature of the time, which intending probation officers read or pretended to read on their training courses, was informed by American models of psycho-social casework (e.g. Monger 1964; Foren and Bailey 1968) and dealt uneasily but at length with the apparent contradiction between the voluntary relationship of therapist and client and the court-mandated relationship between probation officer and offender. (The usual solution to this difficulty was that offenders were too immature to understand their real needs and interests as probation officers did, so the relationship was effectively voluntary even if offenders had not volunteered, because they would have done so if they had been mature enough to understand why they should. This argument could be stated much more convincingly by those who believed in it – see Hunt 1964).

By the end of the 1970s the 'treatment model' was being strongly criticized on a number of empirical and ethical grounds. Empirically, studies of the effectiveness of penal sanctions of all kinds had produced generally discouraging results, and while this was not true of all studies, the general impression that 'nothing works' was reinforced by journalistic summaries (Martinson 1974) and by the overall conclusions of wide-ranging research reviews (Lipton *et al.* 1975; Brody 1976). These findings also gained strength from what were essentially moral or philosophical arguments against 'treatment', such as that it objectified or dehumanized its subjects, or that it rested on unsubstantiated claims of superior professional wisdom (Bottoms and McWilliams 1979). Legal scholars were increasingly questioning whether unreliable predictions about future behaviour should continue to influence sentencing and argued instead for proportionate 'justice' based on the seriousness of the offence (Hood 1974; Von Hirsch 1976). Meanwhile researchers on juvenile justice following the 'treatment'-oriented 1969 Children and Young Persons Act were beginning to document unintended adverse consequences such as increased incarceration following the failure of community-based supervision to prevent further offending (Thorpe *et al.* 1980). It began to appear that young offenders, like their older counterparts, might actually benefit from proportionate 'tariff' sentencing which did not aim to do them good but would at least avoid the excesses of overambitious compulsory 'treatment'. If the emphasis of the 1970s had been on doing good without much success in demonstrating that good was being done, the 1980s were to be about avoiding harm, in particular by reducing unnecessary incarceration. This seemed a more achievable aim, and one which might commend itself on the grounds of economy even to communities or politicians who were not in sympathy with the underlying humanitarian aim. So began the era of 'alternatives to custody': probation was to be a non-custodial penalty aiming to increase its market share and reduce imprisonment, rather than a 'treatment' aiming to change people.

By the end of the 1980s these principles were well enough accepted to be argued in green and white papers (Home Office 1988a, 1990a, 1990b) and embodied in the 1991 Criminal Justice Act, which articulated for the first time in legislation a sentencing rationale based on punishment proportionate to the seriousness of the offence. Probation was to be one of a number of 'community sentences' for those whose offences were serious enough to require a significant sanction but not so serious that only a custodial sentence could be justified. The language of 'alternatives to custody' was now discouraged, but the underlying aim was to make community sentences the standard disposal for middle-range offenders, reserving imprisonment for the most serious or those who presented most risk to the public. Although most probation officers disliked the accompanying rhetoric of 'punishment in the community', which was no doubt intended for public consumption rather than for the professional audience, the Act and the accompanying National Standards paradoxically helped to encourage the next significant shift in probation thinking. The expectation of more frequent contact with supervised offenders and of more demanding and meaningful forms of supervision helped to motivate a search for useful content in supervision programmes.

This search was significantly assisted by an emerging international tendency to question the received wisdom of the 'nothing works' era. Approaches to supervision programme design based on structured social learning, derived for example from psychological approaches to offending behaviour (McGuire and Priestley 1985) and from practice in probation day centres (Vanstone 1993), had already gained some adherents in British probation even if their implementation was often patchy and uneven (Hudson 1988). However, the major challenges to 'nothing works' were emerging from American and Canadian research reviews such as Lipsey (1992) and Andrews *et al.* (1990), and from research in Scotland designed to inform a more effective approach to criminal justice (McIvor 1990). This material, which will be discussed in more detail in Chapter 6, tended, broadly speaking, to favour structured programmes designed to influence attitudes and behaviour, which could be implemented consistently and evaluated. It also offered a realistic prospect of helping some offenders to reduce their offending. A series of publications and 'What Works' conferences gave increasing currency to these ideas (see, for example, McGuire 1995; Underdown 1995), and some probation services began to redefine themselves as providers of potentially effective supervision programmes. This new form of commitment to rehabilitation required some considerable changes in thinking: for example, the new research gave little support to unstructured approaches such as relationship-based reactive counselling when applied to persistent offenders, and this had been the characteristic style of many probation officers. When 'nothing worked' the content of supervision might as well be determined by practitioner preference as by anything else, but the re-emergence of effectiveness required a more critical approach to the content of practice and implied some reduction of practitioners' liberty to practise as they please. Each of these policy shifts both responded to and helped to shape a particular kind of research evidence, which we now review.

Evaluating probation in the 'treatment' era

Reference has already been made to two studies of the late 1950s, Wilkins (1958) and Radzinowicz (1958). These studies were methodologically different, since Radzinowicz documented subsequent offending without comparing it with those subject to other sentences while Wilkins used a comparison group; perhaps not surprisingly, they also came to rather different conclusions about effectiveness, with more negative conclusions in Wilkins's study. However, from the point of view of this chapter it is more interesting to consider where they directed their attention and where they did not. In line with the 'treatment' model, they looked for effects on offenders' subsequent behaviour; they were not interested in criminal justice system issues such as impacts on sentencing, 'market shares' or the tariff level of those supervised. They also appeared to have little interest in the methods used: probation is regarded as a method in itself, and the package is not unwrapped to see what lies inside. The research agenda was confined to the claims of the 'treatment' model and circumscribed by contemporary assumptions about what probation was for, though Wilkins did at least raise the important question of whether probation's effects were measurably better than those of other disposals.

Soon after this the Home Office launched an ambitious programme of research aimed at classifying probationers and their problems empirically, leading to large and interesting studies such as Davies (1969) and eventually to a focus on what probation officers actually did in reponse to these problems (Davies 1974). A significant emerging concern was that probation as psycho-social casework aspired, at least in the textbooks, to a focus on emotional problems (particularly 'underlying' ones) while probationers clearly had many social and environmental difficulties which probation officers addressed to varying degrees, often, according to Davies, without much evidence of resulting change. The agenda was still 'treatment', but anxieties were emerging about the fit between the treatment provided and actual needs. The probation service, of course, could claim that caseloads were too high to allow it to show what it could achieve given better resources, and the eventual response to this was a controlled test, the Intensive Matched Probation and After-Care Treatment (IMPACT) study, which randomly allocated probationers to normal or 'intensive' caseloads and compared both the work done and the subsequent offending in these two groups – a classic research design for testing 'treatment'.

The results of the study (Folkard *et al.* 1976) were discussed remarkably little in the probation service but had a significant effect on the research agenda. The probationers in the experimental small caseloads did receive more attention; the nature of the attention was left to the officers, and could mostly be summarized as more of what they would normally do. The overall results were 'small non-significant differences in reconviction in favour of the control cases', and no confirmation that more probation 'treatment' produced better (or any) effects. The one significant exception was that 'the only experimental cases that apparently do much better are those which have been rated as having low criminal tendencies and which perceive themselves as having many problems', a fairly small group and arguably rather untypical of offenders in general, but broadly resembling offenders who showed positive results in other studies (Adams 1961; Palmer 1974; Shaw 1974). One possible interpretation is that the typical content of probation in the 'treatment' era could be helpful to those who were distressed, anxious to change and not particularly criminal. This prefigured later findings about the limited relevance of relationship-based counselling to work with persistent offenders, but the overall conclusion had to be seen as a negative verdict on probation as a general-purpose 'treatment' for crime: most of the 'culprits' were not being 'readjusted', and the Home Office began to turn its research attention elsewhere. As the Home Office was (and still is) the dominant player in the funding and management of research on the penal system in Britain, this was to have decisive effects on the next decade of British probation research.

Elsewhere, and particularly across the Atlantic, some similar processes were at work, but the more pluralistic research environment allowed the continuation of some research which ran counter to the received orthodoxies of the time. The 1975 research review by Lipton, Martinson and Wilks – which prompted Martinson's (1974) headline-grabbing 'nothing works' article – did not in fact reach uniformly negative conclusions about the studies it examined, and later re-examinations of the same studies – for example by Thornton (1987) – found a number of positive results. Other reviews also began to point to more encouraging conclusions: for example, Blackburn (1980) reviewed a more recent group of studies than those covered by Lipton et al., and found that while few studies met rigorous methodological standards, those which did meet them showed reductions in recidivism. In Canada, Gendreau and Ross (1980) identified a number of studies with positive outcomes and reviewed them as 'bibliotherapy for cynics', an early example of the many positive contributions Canadian researchers were to make to the literature of effective rehabilitation. Perhaps most surprisingly, Martinson (1979) himself published a reappraisal of his earlier conclusion that 'nothing works', arguing that this view was simply incorrect.

The debate, which seemed largely closed in Britain, continued in other countries, with positive findings emerging from Europe (for an early example, see Berntsen and Christiansen 1965) as well as from North America. Even in Britain, some studies showed positive results: for example, enhanced input from prison welfare officers prior to release led, in a well-designed study, to lower reconvictions than in a randomly allocated control group (Shaw 1974) and probation hostels with firm but caring wardens showed less reoffending among their residents than other hostels (Sinclair 1971). However, these results were seen as anomalous and did little, in Britain, to dent the 'nothing works' consensus.

Probation research in the era of diversion

The apparently conclusive demise of 'treatment' produced not only a major shift in policy-makers' views of what probation might realistically achieve but also a corresponding shift in focus for the questions asked by evaluative researchers. The influence of early juvenile justice system studies (e.g. Thorpe *et al.* 1980) has been mentioned already. These studies paid detailed attention to patterns of decision-making in the juvenile courts in an attempt to measure how the activities of social workers were reducing or increasing incarceration, but showed little interest in the content of supervision or the subsequent behaviour of offenders: the guiding assumption seemed to be that post-custodial reconviction rates for juveniles were already so high that any likely outcome of a community-based project would be an improvement. The Home Office itself had already begun to undertake studies guided by a similar set of assumptions about what it was interesting to measure: as well as early work on police cautions which addressed system issues such as net-widening (Ditchfield 1976), a substantial programme of evaluative work on the new community service order had been developing in parallel with the final stages of the probation research programme.

Community service, introduced by the 1972 Criminal Justice Act, was initially implemented on an experimental basis in a number of pilot areas, and the associated Home Office research was primarily concerned with whether it was feasible to implement it; whether courts were using it; and how far it was being used for offenders who would otherwise be sent to prison (Pease *et al.* 1977; Pease and McWilliams 1980). In other words, the community service research agenda was about effects on systems rather than people, and a complete departure from the 'treatment' agenda – so much so that the decision to extend community service to all probation areas was taken before effects on reoffending had been assessed, and issues such as the kinds of help needed or received by offenders and its effects on their behaviour were not addressed until a much later Scottish study (McIvor 1992). Community service was intended to influence sentencers rather than offenders, and the research conformed closely to these priorities; other more rehabilitation-oriented innovations such as the day training centres received far less official research attention (Vanstone and Raynor 1981), and although activities such as social inquiry reports continued to attract interest (Thorpe

1979), government-sponsored research on the effectiveness of probation virtually ceased after IMPACT. One of the few exceptions to this was a short
study of probation day centres (Mair 1988) which revealingly pointed out
that 'it is difficult to assess the success of centres in preventing reoffending;
there is little monitoring of the centres in this respect and the main aim of the
centres is to provide an alternative to custody'. Otherwise the Home Office
Research Studies series during the 1980s was dominated by what has perhaps
too dismissively been described as 'administrative criminology' concerned
with crime prevention, victim surveys and operational issues in criminal justice agencies.

The dominance of new post-treatment, system-centred aims was underlined by the publication in 1984 of a *Statement of National Objectives and
Priorities* (SNOP) for probation services in England and Wales (Home Office
1984). This document, the first attempt at a national statement of the probation service's purpose, was clearly informed by the intention to develop
community-based supervision in such a way as to reduce custodial sentencing. Social inquiry reports were to be a high priority 'where the court may
be prepared to divert an offender from what would otherwise be a custodial
sentence', and probation and community service orders were desirable
'especially in cases where custodial sentences would otherwise be imposed'.
SNOP was in due course accompanied by the introduction of performance
indicators such as the proportion of probationers who were first offenders
(intended to fall) and the proportion with previous custodial experience
(intended to rise). Statistics based on these indicators are still published
annually, long after the policy agenda has moved on, and some of the trends
and developments they reveal are discussed further at the end of this chapter. After-care, presumed to have no diversionary impact, was allocated a
lower place in the order of priorities. Nothing was said about the content or
methods of supervision.

For the probation service itself matters were not so simple. Community
service seemed to be a success, but the market share of probation orders had
been falling throughout most of the 1970s. Probation orders which could be
seen as a credible disposal for more serious offenders would need to offer
more demanding and, if possible, effective programmes of supervision. The
1982 Criminal Justice Act encouraged the inclusion of additional requirements in probation orders to facilitate special programmes, but these larger
packages needed more content. Juvenile justice specialists were already
developing intensive intermediate treatment with often quite sophisticated
programme content (e.g. Denman 1982), and probation services began to
follow suit with various forms of enhanced probation, despite the reservations of some of their staff (Drakeford 1983). Occasionally these involved
an almost bizarre degree of emphasis on control and discipline (Kent Probation and After-Care Service 1981) but more often they looked for content
which seemed likely to be useful to offenders and was intended to reduce

their offending. Among these piecemeal and often unevaluated developments, a few projects took research seriously enough to involve local academics in what became a new style of evaluative study.

Such local projects were typically concerned both with 'market shares' and with impacts on offending, and the combination of modest scale and locally based research allowed for adequate follow-up of both sentencing trends and the behaviour of offenders. Two studies in particular, carried out during the 1980s and published towards the end of the decade (Raynor 1988; Roberts 1989), were able to address some of the issues about effectiveness which had almost vanished from the British research agenda, and in both cases some diversion from custody and some impact on reconviction could be reasonably convincingly demonstrated. One of the studies (Raynor 1988) was also able to document changes in offenders' self-perceived problems and suggested a link between these and subsequent reductions in offending. These attempts to combine the offender-centred concerns of traditional research on effectiveness with the system-centred concerns of the diversion era suggested new and more comprehensive approaches to evaluating probation, some of which we explore in the following chapters.

Other countries were also experimenting with intensive forms of probation. In the United States a variety of schemes were evaluated, often with little to show in the way of diversion from custody or impact on offenders: net-widening was an ever-present danger in a political context which increasingly favoured harsher punishment. However, a good deal was learned about problems of implementation and the importance of the organizational setting (Petersilia 1990). In Canada the continuing interest in psychological approaches to offending was leading to experiments with structured social learning programmes, and these produced some promising results (Ross *et al.* 1988) which encouraged some probation services in Britain to think about running similar programmes. As researchers increasingly moved away from the assumption that 'nothing works' the British government began to outline an enhanced 'centre-stage' role for the probation service in the new policy proposals which were leading towards the 1991 Criminal Justice Act, and the prospects for a more effective and rehabilitative approach to probation began to look brighter than they had for some time.

Some easily forgotten lessons from the past: how diversion succeeded

When awareness of this kind of work eventually impacted on practice and policy in Britain, it led to renewed optimism about the possibility of rehabilitative work with offenders, and in due course to the modern 'What Works' developments discussed in Chapter 6. These changes were to prove so radical, and the political context so different, that there is a risk that some of the positive practice and effects of the era of diversion will simply be forgotten. Partly this is a result of political emphasis: when the then Conservative government was developing the 1991 Criminal Justice Act, a measure to some extent at odds with the repressive and punitive emphasis of some of its other social policies, it clearly intended a reduction in the use of imprisonment. One White Paper described prison as 'an expensive way of making bad people worse' (Home Office 1990a). However, it was believed that the successful promotion of 'community sentences' such as probation and community service required them to be seen as demanding and punitive in their own right ('punishment in the community') rather than simply as alternatives to custody, and instead there was an emphasis on a continuum of penalties embracing both custodial and community-based measures according to the seriousness of the offence, and including penalties served partly in custody and partly in the community (Maguire and Raynor 1997).

Such arrangements required active cooperation between prison and probation services, which was thought unlikely to be achieved if one service continued to define its mission as saving people from the other. Moreover, the first stirrings of a new optimism about rehabilitation were beginning to be felt in the prison service as well as in the probation service: for example, people became aware of Canadian experiments in running prison-based cognitive skills programmes. So, paradoxically, probation services were firmly discouraged by Home Office officials from using the language of 'alternatives to custody': community sentences and prisons were no longer to be in competition, but were targeting different levels of seriousness. In practice, the Act turned out to be genuinely decarcerative, securing unprecedentedly large and rapid reductions in the use of custodial sentences during the few months of 1992 and 1993 in which it was allowed to operate as intended, before politicians shifted their stance and repealed key sections of it. However, the decisive shift away from the language of 'alternatives to custody' turned out to be one of the more enduring legacies of the 1991 Act, to the extent that much of what was learned from successful diversionary research and practice in the 1980s is seldom discussed. This is a mistake, partly because successes in this field are not so common that we can afford to ignore them, and partly because there may be practical lessons to learn or relearn from them.

In essence, the strategies of 'diversion' and 'alternatives to custody' were based on initiatives which started in juvenile justice in England and Wales in the early 1980s (Thorpe et al. 1980) in response to a great increase in the use of custodial sentences and near-custodial forms of residential care for adolescent offenders during the 1970s. The approach which was developed by researchers and particularly practitioners in this field typically involved close analysis of decision-making and case management in local juvenile justice systems in order to promote cautioning, with prosecution only when virtually unavoidable; remands on bail rather than in custody; proposals in social inquiry reports (equivalent to modern pre-sentence reports) for non-custodial sentences, concentrating on the lowest-tariff option for each individual case; avoidance of community sentences in favour of fines and discharges in non-serious cases; and the development of enhanced programmes of supervision to offer to the courts in cases where these would be the only realistic alternative to a custodial sentence.

This approach did in fact achieve a substantial reduction in custodial sentencing of young offenders during the 1980s (Smith 1995) and helped to facilitate the reductions in residential care for young people which were also being sought by local authorities on financial grounds. The practitioners who made these approaches work mostly shared an orientation to adolescent offending which can be summed up in the idea of 'growing out of crime' (Rutherford 1986): they saw adolescent offending as a phase which would normally end as part of a maturation process, and they developed practice designed to avoid over-reaction and deviancy amplification in response to a temporary 'drift' into delinquency – as described long before by Matza (1964). A more realistic view, based on the information about criminal careers which is now available from cohort studies (e.g. Farrington 1990) would be that about half of known male adolescent offenders could fairly be described as 'adolescence-limited'; others are likely to continue into adult offending and develop a pattern of recidivism. However, an orientation which emphasized normalization and the likelihood of maturation probably did less harm than seeing adolescent offending as always a sign of deep-seated problems which available methods of supervision were as likely to aggravate as to alleviate. Although arguably under-reacting to the problems presented by some persistent young offenders, the approach represented an early example of an empirically based strategy which achieved at least some of the intended results – a precursor of 'What Works'.

How diversion worked with adults and was then abandoned

The agencies dealing with adult offenders were slower to see the potential of this approach, and never adopted it to the same degree as bodies like the Association for Juvenile Justice, probably because the problems of seriousness and persistence presented by some adults were not so easily marginalized and the adult system was traditionally more retributive. However, the emergence of a near-consensus around the idea of probation as an alternative to custody reflected similar thinking, just as the earliest probation service 'specified activity' programmes were influenced by earlier work undertaken with juveniles under the label of 'intermediate treatment'. As we have already noted, SNOP (Home Office 1984) required probation services to give the highest priority to providing credible forms of supervision in the community for courts to use for offenders who would otherwise have received custodial sentences, and to recommend these disposals to sentencers in realistic and persuasive reports: 'the first priority should be to ensure that, wherever possible, offenders can be dealt with by non-custodial measures and that standards of supervision are set and maintained at the level required for this purpose' (p. 5). In addition, new statistical performance indicators were devised to see how far probation services were achieving this: in particular, they were to make routine returns on the proportion of probation orders and community service orders being made in respect of offenders who had previously served a prison sentence, and the proportion in respect of people with no previous convictions.

This did in fact work: both indicators moved fairly steadily in the intended direction during the remainder of the 1980s. In 1993 43 per cent of new probationers in that year had experienced custodial sentences, and in 1991 only 11 per cent of them were first offenders. Community service orders made in 1989 showed 37 per cent former prisoners and 14 per cent first offenders, and the first full year of combination orders in 1993 saw 49 per cent of them used for people who had experienced imprisonment and 10 per cent used for first offenders. This was also a period of low imprisonment by current standards (particularly low in 1992–93) and substantial use of fines. These were, by any standards, significant achievements. By 1999, the position was rather different: only 34 per cent of probation orders were made on people with custodial experience (although there must have been more such people around than in previous years) and 24 per cent were on first offenders. The equivalent figures for community service in 1999 were 20 per cent with custodial experience and a striking 42 per cent first offenders (well over double the 1989 figure), while combination orders in 1999 showed 34 per cent with custodial experience and 23 per cent first offenders. Combination orders were also increasing in number, while community service orders declined (Home Office 2000a).

The changes since the late 1980s and early 1990s are evident, and in a consistent direction. It is no surprise to see that they coincide with unprecedented growth in imprisonment and a marked reduction in the use of fines. Obviously the sentencing climate and the legislation have changed, but there seems also to have been a shift from promoting non-custodial sentencing as a preferred option for those at the lower end of the custodial range, to marketing community sentences wherever a market can be found. During most of the 1990s this was encouraged by a funding model based on volume, which may have provided a perverse incentive to go after as many orders as possible; but what is worrying is how quickly the lessons of the 1980s were unlearned and perceived as no longer relevant. What happened to the concerns about 'net-widening' or exposing people to higher-tariff sanctions than necessary, which were part of everyday probation language during the 1980s? There are also other grounds for concern: for example, such figures do not obviously support probation services' contention that their caseloads are growing more and more 'risky', though that may be more true of post-custodial 'through-care' supervision. The practices revealed by these figures also appear questionable in relation to the 'risk principle' that programmes of supervision are less likely to be effective when used for low-risk offenders (Andrews *et al.* 1990), and in relation to long-standing research findings that male first offenders put on probation were twice as likely to be reconvicted as male first offenders who were fined (Walker *et al.* 1981).

More recently and perhaps more controversially, Feeley and Simon (1992) have suggested that there is

> a tendency in courts and other social agencies toward decoupling performance evaluation from external social objectives . . . such technocratic rationalization tends to insulate institutions from the messy, hard-to-control demands of the social world. By limiting their exposure to indicators that they can control, managers ensure that their problems will have solutions.

In other words, if you are in a difficult environment it may be attractive to go simply for *more* community sentences rather than for the more difficult task of persuading sentencers to make the *right* community sentences, particularly if your funding regime encourages you to behave in this way. It would be difficult, however, to infer from the 1999 probation statistics (Home Office 2001) exactly what the social mission of the probation service is, or what its distinctive principled contribution to criminal justice is meant to be. The 1991 Criminal Justice Act failed to survive political pressures; the probation service's own bruising encounter with those same pressures left it in need of a new clarity and some restatement of mission.

This chapter has shown how research began, in the 1970s, to pose a real challenge to the probation service of the time. However, it has also shown the probation service blown about by the changeable weather of criminal justice politics; the acts of collective remembering which create the tradition and culture of a public institution have been balanced by acts of collective forgetting when situational pressures required something new, and research which was itself shaped by and responsive to the same pressures could not provide a continuing point of reference. The underlying lesson of the 1980s and their aftermath may be that the probation service has not succeeded in behaving as the kind of 'learning organization' it has aspired to be. Under political pressure it has 'unlearned', and shown itself to be reactive to political and cultural environment rather than a confident and independent source of convincing ideas about its own role and function.

The successes of the 1980s were not in any way a complete answer, but they needed to be learned from and built on rather than simply disowned when they became politically inconvenient. The next two chapters will focus on the pressures of populist punitiveness and on the probation service's attempt to find a response in evidence-based practice or 'what works'. In this we begin to see the possibility of a genuinely reflective, curious, self-critical and learning service: the pressures will not be less, but the resources for responding to them will be far greater if the promise of the evidence-based approach is fully developed and used. It is to be hoped that one benefit of the evidence-based approach will be a more cumulative and confident approach to learning and to the development of professional knowledge.

Further reading

Raynor (1985) and Bottoms and McWilliams (1979) are very good sources for students looking for illustrations of the literature of the period described in this chapter.

chapter five

Too soft on criminals? Community sentences and populist punitiveness

The emergence of evidence that working with offenders in the community can be effective in reducing their offending has in some respects been overshadowed by the fact that during the last decade of the twentieth century the number of people imprisoned rose in Britain to levels that even a decade earlier would have been regarded as symptoms of a crisis within the system. In a relatively short period the debate about prisons had shifted from the post-war consensus about the deleterious effect of imprisonment to a 'prison works' rhetoric; and from the ameliorative tones of the Woolf (1991) report to the punitive populism of Michael Howard, the Conservative Home Secretary. A cursory analysis of these changes produces an illusionary sense of a sudden spasm of atavistic punitive urges, and a casual rejection of consensus. However, the picture is much more complicated than that, and the sharp rise in the prison population can be seen partly as a culmination of a process of the politicization of crime that had begun to gain its momentum almost half a century earlier, and partly as a result of growth of recorded crime. It must be remembered that although the number of people in prison at the end of the century was high relative to the level of the 1970s and 1980s, the person who committed a crime in 1950 had a chance of going to prison that was about double what it is today. This makes the discussion in this chapter about what in some senses is a drift to a more punitive criminal justice (more people go to prison and for longer) much more complicated. Consequently, in this chapter we examine the context of this drift; and in doing so we relate this development to wider political and cultural changes, and in particular to the anti-collectivist tendency to seek to regulate the poor through law enforcement as opposed to empowering them through welfare. However, we also attempt a critique of the morality of sending people to prison. This will lead us through an examination of how 'law and order' has become a political issue; the collapse of the 'rehabilitative ideal' and its displacement by the 'eliminative ideal' (Rutherford 1993); the penal crisis of the 1980s; and the redefining of community sentences as 'punishment in the community', together with the construction of new forms of accountability and regulation to ensure the adoption of the new agenda by practitioners. It is a central argument of this chapter that the direction of policy and practice in the supervision of community sentences has, in part at least, been shaped by these phenomena.

The politicization of crime

Although populist concerns about disorder and crime are not new (Pearson 1983; Taylor 1998), during the past fifty years there has been an unprecedented rise in the degree to which crime-related problems have entered into political and popular discourse. No doubt the expansion of the media has played its part; in particular, it has promulgated what Beckett (1997) describes as the 'democracy at work thesis', namely that there is a kind of symbiotic relationship between a worsening crime problem and public sentiment. In arguing that the relationship between public perception of crime problems and attitudes towards punishment is both fluid and complex, she offers an alternative version of the story behind the ascendance of the 'get tough' approach to crime. In her view, crime issues are constructed both politically and socially by elite 'claimsmakers' who wield power in order to gain acceptance of their preferred interpretations. The success of 'claimsmakers' depends on access to sympathetic media, a range of symbols and rhetoric that 'resonate with deep-seated myths' and make sense of people's day-to-day experiences and an apposite historical moment rather than the evidence of research. What Beckett has to say about America has its resonance in the British experience. There, too, for much of the twentieth century 'penological modernism', underpinned by the belief that crime was at least partly caused by socio-economic factors, formed the basis of criminal justice and social welfare practice aimed at rehabilitation. The vacuum created by the demise of rehabilitation as a viable goal of state intervention was filled, according to Beckett, on the one hand by politicians and their agenda of deterrence, retribution and public safety, and on the other hand by the growth of the new penology underpinned by administrative and managerial imperatives. The practitioners of criminal justice became the means of controlling troublesome individuals, and politicians used crime-related issues to manipulate public opinion.

By examining the links between political initiatives, media coverage, public concern about crime and the crime rate in America between 1964 and 1974, Beckett demonstrates that the first two were closely associated with levels of public concern while the reported incidence of crime was not. Furthermore, she shows that more recently, between 1985 and 1992, political initiatives on drugs were closely associated with public concern about drugs whereas the actual reported incidence of drug use was not. Overall, her examination of the number of political initiatives and poll results through the 1960s, 1970s and 1980s shows that public concern and political initiatives move in similar directions. She also challenges the conventional view of the relationship between increased public concern and punitive attitudes by, for instance, rehearsing evidence that rates of victimization among black people are greater than among white people but that whites are more supportive of punitive policies.

So, how and why are crime-related issues defined by political elites as problems of insufficient punishment and control or as being 'soft' on criminals? Beckett traces the history in America through the FBI clampdown on immigration and political dissent in the 1920s and their diminution as issues in the 1950s; from their re-emergence in the political protests of the early 1960s through to the 1964 Goldwater right-wing election campaign; from the civil rights movement to the 1968 election and the politics of law and order and the subsequent populism of the New Right. This may be an accurate picture of the process in America, but how if at all does it relate to Britain and of what relevance is it to our understanding of the supervision of offenders in the community?

The first British election manifesto to contain law and order as an issue was that of the Conservatives in 1959, and since that time it has moved increasingly to the fore as a political concern (Downes and Morgan 1997). The period between 1945 and the 1959 election was characterized by what Rawlings (1999: 122) calls 'the march of the liberal progressives'. As argued by Downes and Morgan, the task of rebuilding the economy and social structure of Britain after the Second World War led to a consensus among the political parties (Butskellism) premised on a commitment to the welfare state: in comparison, crime was not a focus of direct concern. In their examination of party manifestos and election campaigns, Downes and Morgan demonstrate how first the Conservatives in 1959 and then Labour in 1966 focused attention on crime-related issues, and continued to do so with increasing partisanship through the 1970s. The Conservative Party attacked the Labour government for presiding over rising crime and violence, but more significantly linked crime to industrial disputes and other threats to social order, thus providing a parallel to the trend in America identified by Beckett. As a consequence, they suggest, by the mid-1970s 'law and order issues . . . assume as much prominence in major party election manifestos as, for example, housing, transport and urban renewal' (Downes and Morgan 1997: 189). However, it is the 1979 election that they identify as the watershed in the successful exploitation by the Conservatives of crime as a politically attuned electioneering device. Their success is attributed to their merging of crime and industrial disorder following the 'winter of discontent'. A pattern was established for the last quarter of the century, with, on the one hand, Labour relating the reduction of crime to the elimination of poverty and racism, and on the other hand, the Conservatives linking it to extra police, tougher sentencing and legislation on issues like secondary picketing and immigration control. In a telling summation, Downes and Morgan (1997: 225) assert that 'the "hostages to fortune" which Labour Party attachments to the trade unions and to libertarian causes entail, have led its leaders to seek to neutralize, rather than sharply contest, the Conservative hegemony on this issue'.

In his introduction to the theoretical and political history of non-custodial sentencing, Brownlee (1998) argues that the contextual shift from integration and inclusion to separation and exclusion has not been accidental but rather the result of political decisions and policies increasingly shaped by a response to supposed public opinion. We agree but are inclined to the view that public opinion is increasingly shaped by the level of political activity – through politicians and media – surrounding crime-related issues.

Paradoxically, Conservative populism disguised more pragmatic, liberal policy developments. It was the Conservatives who introduced both community service and day training centres, both alternatives to custody; it was a Conservative home secretary (Kenneth Clarke) who responded to a prison overcrowding problem by introducing half sentence remission; it was another who acknowledged prisons as universities of crime (Douglas Hurd); and it was the Conservative Party that brought in the radical 1991 Criminal Justice Act, which introduced the principle of people being fined according to their means (so-called 'unit fines'), and proscribed, in most circumstances, the consideration of previous convictions in sentencing (Section 29). Admittedly, both were quickly repealed in response to pressure from sentencers and other pressure groups, but it was not until the appointment of Michael Howard that populist rhetoric was more overtly fused with populist policy: his 27-point get-tough plan, prompted by events such as the IRA bomb in London's Bishopsgate, the murder of Jamie Bulger and the supposed threat from New Age travellers, was followed by the 1994 Criminal Justice and Public Order Act and the inevitable increase in the numbers being sent to prison (Rawlings 1999).

This process of politicization, then, had reached its high point, and its companion social authoritarianism had unified the political right and left (Scraton 1987; Drakeford and Vanstone 2000). Moreover, as Downes and Morgan (1997) have argued, crime had been linked indelibly to the issue of industrial and social disorder. This, of course, is not new; fear of social breakdown has underpinned criminal justice responses since the eighteenth century (Ignatieff 1978; Pearson 1983; Taylor 1998). However, it is in its modern manifestation and the context it has created for community sentences that we are interested here.

From inclusion to exclusion: the new political order

The foci of the 'social authoritarianism' of the incoming Conservative government of 1979 were, according to Scraton (1987), offenders, the 'immoral', the excessively powerful trade unions, welfare spongers and the feckless who would not work. The new agenda of the right involved regulation through the law; increased pay and resources for the police and armed forces; a special unit to reduce benefit fraud; and more punitive sentencing symbolized by the notion of the 'short, sharp shock' regime of detention centres for young offenders and by longer prison sentences. A corollary to this attack on welfarism, Scraton argues, was an increase in racism and a failure on the part of the government to take it seriously. This shift in political activity has been described variously as a change from the pursuit of social justice to criminal justice and the prioritizing of social control over social welfare (Hudson 1993; Arnold and Jordan 1996); an increase in state discipline (Walker and Beaumont 1985); and the promotion of 'individualism, familialism and nationalism' at the expense of increasingly marginalized minority groups (Worrall 1997: 22).

As a basic description of what has become known as 'Thatcherism', this conflation of these various accounts is adequate. But it does obscure a more complex story of the enactment of criminal justice policy during the 1980s and early 1990s. A clue to this can be found in the argument by some that a new penological discourse with emphasis on the identification and managing of unruly groups emerged from these policies (Feeley and Simon 1992). The main features of this discourse, they argue, are new techniques such as electronic monitoring systems and prediction scales; risk assessment; a sentencing continuum of prison for high risk to probation for low risk; more penal sanctions; a higher prison population; increase in the use of probation and early release; and expansion of control. Moreover, in their introduction to the notion of a new, more realistic view of the problem of crime (left realism), Young and Matthews (1992: 2) point out that 'Thatcherite policy has been diverse, uneven, and at times clearly contradictory'. As evidence of this they point to the fact that the toughening up of sentencing for some categories of offender was accompanied by increases in cautioning and diversion from custody for other categories; increased prison building was paralleled by a slowdown in the increase of the prison population; and fiscal concerns tempered the political instinct for punitiveness. In a direct challenge to the analysis of commentators like Scraton, they argue that:

> [t]hese paradoxes of policy suggest that it would be incorrect to see recent government policy in Britain as involving simply the exercise of increased repression or as representing a form of 'authoritarian populism' [and that neither] of these terms adequately captures the vicissitudes of recent right-wing policies, and consequently they offer little help in understanding, combating or providing alternatives to these policies. (p. 3)

While some might argue that they may be overstating their case as a reaction to the very real problems faced by left-wing criminologists in the face of, for instance, growing awareness of victim perspectives (some understanding of the ideology of right-wing policies is provided by the term 'social authoritarianism'), they do highlight the complexity of the history of policy development. The unravelling of that complexity is helped by reference to some other narratives.

The *extension of control* thesis has been applied to the general development of social and penal policy and not simply to the Thatcher government. Cohen (1985) has argued that the discipline of the prison has been dispersed into the community through policies of decarceration, which have extended the network of social control. This has occurred first through alternatives to custody drawing into the system those who were not in danger of a custodial sentence in the first place (widening the net); second, by increasing the amount of intervention through extra conditions in community sentences (thinning the mesh); third, by obscuring the distinction between institutions and non-institutions, for example day training centres (blurring); and lastly, by the extension of social control to informal societal networks, for example, foster families (penetration). The net effect of these processes, Cohen argues graphically, has been a widening of the 'carceral archipelago'. Mathiesen (1983) extends this interpretation by highlighting the increase of general surveillance and covert discipline through such means as closed-circuit television cameras, an increase in private security firms and extra police. This *dispersal of discipline* thesis has been challenged, at least in part, by Bottoms (1983) who asserts that it confuses surveillance with discipline, ignores the reparative and compensatory elements of some sentences and fails to take into account rehabilitative efforts. Vanstone (1993) has argued the latter point also in reference to the motivations of probation officers and others who worked in projects concerned with alternatives to custody during the 1970s and 1980s. He suggests that Cohen fails to take account of the fact that many of those practitioners, far from extending discipline, diluted it with liberal doses of attempted rehabilitation.

Young (1999) provides a very useful overarching and, in some senses, unifying analysis of the changes alluded to in the above accounts. He traces what he describes as the shift from modernity, characterized by assimilation and incorporation of 'outgroups' in society, to late modernity, characterized by their separation and exclusion. The social contract of modernity has, in his view, broken down not simply because of the imposition of a new hegemonic political orthodoxy, but because 'it was ill conceived [and] in part because the world has changed' (p. 197). In his version of the 'modernist project', the status of citizenship was achieved through an emphasis on social equality, and social equality was striven for through a commitment to social justice. Moreover, the deviant was a person whose criminality was to be investigated and whose rehabilitation was to be sought; a consensus existed about the need for social order, collective responsibility and the aim of assimilation; and the majority of people conformed to this consensual view of behaviour. In contrast, late modernity, prefigured by the economic crises of the 1960s and 1970s and the demise of 'Fordism', is infused with the hegemony of market forces and individualism in a pluralistic society shaped by diverse lifestyles. Within this society, everyone is a potential deviant whose level of threat is the subject of actuarial concern, rising crime is paralleled by increased exclusion by incarceration (what Rutherford terms the 'eliminative ideal'), and there is a retreat from collective responsibility. The direction in which late modernity might be taking us is the creation of what Young vividly describes as an 'exclusive dystopia' which has a central core of people who are employed and have a clear stake in society, albeit one increasingly threatened by less job security (what New Labour might call stakeholders); a cordon sanitaire between the core and those on the outside, patrolled by various devices of the state; and the outgroup or underclass who 'live in idleness and crime' (p. 20). One further feature of late modernity is critical to the completion of this description of the historical context of community sentences in the late twentieth century, namely what some observers have labelled the penal crisis of the 1980s.

The penal crisis

The loss of faith in the rehabilitative ideal has already been traced in earlier chapters, but it is revisited in this chapter as a component of the penal crisis. The more general context of what some commentators have described as the penal crisis (Cavadino and Dignan 1997) is best depicted by Garland's (1985, 1990) analysis of the problem of punishment in the second half of the twentieth century. His contention is that the problem can be broken down into component parts. First, the role of punishment has become unclear, so that there is both uncertainty about whether it is meant, for instance, to protect the public or to rehabilitate the offender or to reduce crime by deterrence, and doubt about whether in certain cases it has a role at all.[1] Second, the structure of punishment is taken for granted.[2] Third, as has been suggested earlier in the chapter, the politicization of crime as an issue has contributed to constrained and narrow thinking; put another way, punitive populism increasingly has determined the agenda of the discourse of punishment. Finally, that discourse has been adjusted to a framework that is largely unchallenged.

So, according to Garland's thesis the institutions of punishment tell us what criminality is, how it will be sanctioned, the proportions of appropriate punishment and who is entitled to administer it. The overriding questions are predicated on concerns about private or state control of prisons; security versus humanity; management and administration; and whether probation should be welfare or punishment. What Garland calls 'the regime of truth' eschews questions such as whether we should use prison as a punishment, and what a severe punishment is. Authoritative experts, driven themselves by historical convention and the self-justification of the institutions within which they work, determine what happens. This is truer, perhaps, of prison than of community sentences. Periodically, the efficacy of prisons has been challenged by the powerful – Home Secretary Douglas Hurd, for instance, at the end of the 1980s – but prison officials do not have to plead the case of imprisonment as a sentence. On the other hand, alternatives to prison, such as probation with special conditions and community service, have undergone constant scrutiny of their effectiveness (see, for example, McIvor 1991; Hedderman and Sugg 1997; Mair 1997), and in presentence reports probation officers have to make their case for such sentences. The prison survives because it is there, because of its symbolic status and because it has a cocooned existence. Admittedly, Garland does list the features of a decline in optimism about punishment – rising crime, prison unrest and a loss of faith in rehabilitation – and for a period between the prison riots of the early 1980s and the Woolf (1991) report prison was in the dock with other sentences. However, at the beginning of the twenty-first century it remains relatively free of the effects of the declining confidence in rehabilitation, while community sentences face the brunt of criticism. Of course, it is true that until very recently rehabilitation had been discontinued as an objective of prison regimes,[3] but prison still had credibility as a punishment. Community sentences, on the other hand, despite attempts to inculcate them with punishment, have only rehabilitative effort on which to found their credibility.

To a degree, Garland describes what might be judged a crisis but he couches it more in terms of one about the concept of punishment. Cavadino and Dignan (1997) apply the description to the penal system as a whole, and by implication the criminal justice system too. In their analysis, the penal system can be perceived as having reached a point at the end of the 1980s of either moral danger to society or a critical need for change. They iterate Garland's assessment of dysfunction in terms of failed community sentences and custodial sentences; high financial cost; and low confidence in the chances of any sentence having a positive impact on future offending. They ascribe a number of features to this crisis: first, prison riots culminating in the devastating uprising in Strangeways prison in 1990; second, the Woolf (1991) report which emerged from political and societal concerns about the unrest; third, the Conservative administration's 'law and order' ideology (ironically, a policy that was to appear positively benign compared to that of the later Home Secretary, Michael Howard); the Criminal Justice Act 1991 and its hybrid version of 'just deserts'; and finally, the 'counter-revolution' and its repeal of unit fines and Section 29 of the Criminal Justice Act 1991.

Cavadino and Dignan helpfully elaborate a number of different accounts of the crisis before adding their own. The first of these is the orthodox account, which cites a combination of a high prison population resulting from government policies, court decisions and a bifurcated sentencing strategy; overcrowding and bad conditions in prisons; understaffing and unrest among staff; poor security; a 'potent mix' of less serious offenders with more serious; and riots and a failure of control. The second is the radical account, which includes these features but puts emphasis on five aspects: conditions; containment; the undermining of the authority of staff; a decrease in the legitimacy of prisons caused by increased exposure to public scrutiny; and charges of being over-indulgent schools of crime. Next is the critical mainstream account, which gives weight to the collapse of the rehabilitative ideal; the erosion of the rehabilitative goal of prison and increased emphasis on management and control; the size of the prison population and bifurcation.[4] Finally, there is the Woolf diagnosis which followed the Strangeways prison riots, centred on security, control and justice. In essence, Woolf argued that the increase in concern about security and discipline had added to prisoners' sense of injustice, and he recommended, among other things, a reform of the grievance procedures and disciplinary processes; better conditions; preparation for release that helped to stop offending; and community prisons. While accepting many of the elements of these accounts, Cavadino and Dignan put forward what they call a composite and compromise theory. Their 'radical and pluralist' analysis takes account of the fact that the crisis involved, and we would argue still involves, a number of varied factors and interest groups with differing degrees of power. They correctly place their examination of the crisis in the context of politics and economics, ideology and material conditions. These dimensions impose themselves on the process of articulation within the debate, and highlight a parallel context for the developments during this period of community sentences.

In our view, while the moral dimension to the crisis in these accounts is implicit, it needs to be made explicit. The issue is not just about how many

sent to prison, in what conditions and whether the process is effec-
(although these are obviously important questions) but also about the
moral justification for punishing people through the use of custody. The
application of a moral test of the decision to imprison someone would neces-
sitate consideration of such things as the unintended consequences of the
sentence, the moral culpability of the offender, and the balance between the
proportion of harm caused by the offence and that caused by the sentence.
We are not arguing that the consideration of such matters in sentencing is
new, but rather that they need to be reaffirmed as relevant factors. So, the
impact of a person's incarceration on others would have to be judged in
terms of collateral victimization: for instance, is the custodial sentence
justified if the offender's children are likely to be deprived, emotionally dam-
aged and/or stigmatized as a result? Furthermore, a consideration of
whether the harm caused by the offence is outweighed by the possible harm
caused by the sentence might lead to a judgement that certain offences could
never lead to a prison sentence. We recognize that judgements about harm
are likely to be extremely difficult to make; for instance, a very similar
offence can have quite different effects on different people – theft from a
poor person might cause more hardship than that from a better-off person,
but it might cause more emotional damage to the latter. Nevertheless, difficult though it may be, the moral dimension of sentencing has to be included
in the process of sentencing to custody; simply asking 'does it work?' is not
enough. The same is true of community sentences.

The rehabilitation of community sentences

Our understanding of the direction that community sentencing has taken at
the outset of the twenty-first century is dependent on insight into the ideological and political force field of debate and discourse. During a relatively
short period a number of ideological models have been revisited – rehabilitation, just deserts, radicalism, incapacitation and general deterrence, and
reparation. The first, as indicated earlier in this book, found its impetus from
the work of Ross et al. (1988) and others in Britain (McGuire 1995; Raynor
and Vanstone 1997) centred on the cognitive-behavioural model (Vanstone
2000); the second found expression, albeit in a hybrid form, in the Criminal
Justice Act 1991 and was premised on the notions that offending is a matter
of opportunity and conscious choice, that the offender is an accountable
moral agent, and that the severity of the sentencing response is determined
by the seriousness of the offence. The third was based on the contention that
as long as there is social injustice and discrimination there can be no criminal justice. The fourth assumed its most graphic form in the 'three strikes'
policy in some American states and was stimulated by a pessimism about
human nature and optimism about the protective effect of incarceration.

The fifth emerged in a non-direct form with the introduction of community service in Britain in the early 1970s and the more direct form of offender–victim mediation and reparation schemes of the 1980s and 1990s, and was based on the principle of redressing harm.

Hudson (1993) has provided a succinct and illuminating analysis of the process that emerged from this complex ideological interplay. She describes a drift from reforming to penalizing, in which the rehabilitation of the individual offender gives way to the administering of consistent punishment; from social science to legal science, in which assessment of risk supplants prescription of treatment; and from the normalizing to the actuarial regime, in which those who present a risk to the public are segregated and watched over, thus widening the gap between the 'deviant' and the 'normal'. It is not as clear-cut as that; Hudson is merely trying to characterize broad trends and does not ignore the fact that rehabilitation has survived, as has the social science that informs it. The point is that it has done so in a changed political and social climate and as a result has assumed a different shape. Much of that change, we argue, has been positive; for instance, the shift towards evidence-based practice. However, it has been at some cost, and in order to assess those benefits and costs it is necessary to summarize the history of change.

A more accountable Service

As we have outlined earlier, before 1984 the probation service had survived in a relatively benign political and social world. Its efforts, by and large, were accepted as justified in their own right, and lack of evidence of effectiveness proved to be no barrier to the implementation of rehabilitative effort in a number of guises. Its policies and practices were rather loosely regulated. This began to change with the issue by the government of SNOP (Home Office 1984). This inaugurated an eventful period in the history of the probation service which involved a search for more effective ways to reduce reoffending, and an increase in the impact on probation policy and practice of new variations and forms of accountability, accompanied by the new managerialism of public sector management practice and criminal justice policy (Humphrey and Pease 1992; Raynor 1997).

SNOP attempted for the first time to regulate the policy and practice direction of the probation service at a national level. May (1991b) has argued that the attempt to introduce a justice model in the early 1990s was dependent on the greater 'centralized state activity' that SNOP introduced, but at the time many probation officers viewed it as a major threat to the traditional purpose of the service (Mair 1997). Until then local services had enjoyed considerable autonomy from central government, and this had been perceived by many as a strength; so, if not a threat, SNOP was certainly the watershed described by Mair in so far as it was interventionist and it placed a responsibility on chief probation officers to ensure that their services were cost-efficient. This latter development led to a change in the culture of the services, which had a direct impact at the level of practice because it was bound up with a set of prescribed priorities (May 1991b). The service was required, first, to provide alternatives to custody; second, to prepare what were then called social inquiry reports; third, to resource the throughcare of prisoners to ensure that statutory requirements were met; fourth, to work in the community; and fifth, to provide sufficient resources to civil work. These gave a clear message about what the service should concentrate on, and in retrospect can be seen to have prefigured a highly significant change in the direction of both policy and practice. According to one commentator, 'the attention of local services was directed to the "bifurcated" policy objectives signalled in the Criminal Justice Act 1982 of increased diversion of some offenders and new, more punitive responses to others' (Brownlee 1998: 86). The policy of diverting people from custody was, however, to have a relatively short shelf life, and rehabilitation was to receive a kiss of life, but the days of probation officers implementing 'varied and sometimes unstated organizational goals' (May 1991b: 44) were over; increasingly probation personnel were having to negotiate the 'shifting sands of working with offenders' (May and Vass 1996).

It might be overstating it to suggest that probation services resisted the attempt at centralized regulation, but some did set their own local objectives and variations remained (Worrall 1998). However, the tide had changed and the inexorable process continued with attempts by the Home Office to exert influence in the form of a series of papers designed to regulate policy and practice (Home Office 1988a, 1988b, 1990a, 1990b, 1992). These papers were informed by the view that the probation service needed to take a more offence-centred view of its supervisory tasks and that community sentences could be more effective than prison in reducing reoffending, as well as being significantly cheaper. Underpinning these prescriptions was an optimism about effectiveness rather tenuously based on a few, untypical evaluative studies available in Britain (Raynor 1988; Roberts 1989); and thus it marked the end of the dominance of the 'nothing works' view (Martinson 1974; Brody 1976). It seemed clear that probation services in the future would be judged by the effectiveness of their impact on offending rather than by their success in diverting offenders from custody, and this new approach to probation's purposes and potential led directly to the search for methods of supervision which could make evidence-based claims of potential effectiveness. That search took place alongside other significant changes in the political context within which the service now found itself.

The search for effective programmes was accompanied by an increase in demands for accountability and the Financial Management Initiative that had been applied to other parts of the public sector. These demands were facilitated by the further refinement of information technology first introduced into the probation service in the mid-1980s. In 1992, National Standards were introduced for the first time, and these were seen (depending on the political ideology of the observer) as a necessary corollary to the quest for improved practice or a narrow, bureaucratic device to ensure the standardization of mediocrity. Moreover, the optimism was suddenly curtailed by the 'prison works' doctrine of a new Home Secretary in 1993. As a result, the last years of the Conservative government were characterized by punitive populism, scepticism and some hostility towards the traditional assumptions of probation practice (see Chapter 2), and training for probation officers in a social work context was abolished (Williams 1995, 1996).

Although the process had begun earlier the change in training might be seen as a very significant symbol of the change from a court welfare service to a corrections agency. Debate in the probation service certainly assumed a greater urgency, but the response to these changes was not uniform. Some probation officers and commentators were antagonistic towards and sceptical about this new populism and its 'tough' language about punishment in the community (Drakeford 1983; Rumgay 1989). Rumgay, in particular, argued that the use of the aggressive language of punishment would ultimately change practice and the values upon which it was based, and many people within the service agreed. Others accepted change in language as a necessary part of the move to increase the credibility of community sentences, to counter the *soft option* tag, as it were. Both arguments have a point. The way that people describe their behaviour can mould that behaviour, and, as we have already argued, community supervision should not be *for* punishment. But the introduction of the phrase *punishment in the community* might indeed have been the beginning of a twin-track policy in the Home Office: one rhetoric for the public and some sections of the press, and another for the professionals.

The tensions evident in the debate about language also existed between the practice culture of the probation service and the incipient management culture. It was, after all, being driven by a government that had pursued a market philosophy that had led to increases in unemployment and reductions in income support (Stewart *et al.* 1994). On the one hand, there was an autonomous practice culture jaded by 'nothing works' research and detached from evaluation, and, on the other hand, the new managerialism (McWilliams 1990), greater accountability and demands for evidence about effectiveness. In addition, there were some voices in the service arguing for a revised value base that more accurately represented the practices and policies of the service as it approached the end of the century (Nellis 1995). Furthermore, just as there was conflict among those with an interest in how community sentences were managed and delivered, so there were tensions within the processes of change. For instance, it is not at all clear that new managerialism and the implications of the emerging knowledge base about effectiveness were concordant; National Standards (Home Office 1992, 1995a) focus far more on regulation and procedure than they do on 'what works' research evidence.

However, it was the fact that change to probation officers' traditional autonomy was demanded by the exigencies of greater effectiveness and accountability that stimulated a sceptical approach to research-based developments from practitioners and some academics (e.g. Pitts 1992; Jones *et al.* 1992). That scepticism remained at the end of the twentieth century (Worrall 2000), but it had become increasingly difficult for any practitioners to resist the demands for evidence-based practice. The newly incumbent Labour government seemed more inclined to listen to the voice of research (Hedderman and Sugg 1997; Goldblatt and Lewis 1998), and in 1998 the Home Office issued Circular 35/1998 and launched the Effective Practice Initiative (Home Office 1998) which was drawn from agreement between Home Office ministers, the Association of Chief Probation Officers and the Home Office Inspectorate of Probation. In what can be seen as the culmination of a long process of government regulation, it stated that all probation services should 'ensure that every offender is supervised in accordance with those principles which have been shown to reduce expected rates of re-offending' (Home Office 1998). The supervision of community sentences by practitioners informed by evidence of what was likely to be most effective in helping people to desist from offending was the goal, state-sponsored research and accreditation of programmes were to be the means.

Conclusion

The last quarter of the twentieth century, therefore, witnessed a significant and far-reaching change in the political and cultural context of the community supervision of offenders. Increasingly, crime became a political issue and therefore vulnerable to the vicissitudes of changing political values and priorities. In turn, those changes, combined with the increasingly atavistic appetite of the popular press, stimulated the emergence of a social culture characterized by exclusive rather than inclusive instincts, and the cult of dangerousness. Riots and an official inquiry had subjected prison to a temporary challenge to its legitimacy as a primary punishment, but it had then recovered its traditional and symbolic position as the emblem of society's virility in dealing with crime. Meanwhile, community supervision had been transmuted into punishment in the community, the implementation of which was driven by managerialist imperatives, not wholly or necessarily negative in effect. The demands of accountancy were balanced by accountability premised on evidence-based practice, leaving a glimmer of hope for the future viability of community supervision. The next chapter reviews the current state of the research upon which evidence-based practice rests, and gives an account of the emergence of cognitive-behavioural and pro-social models as methodological expressions of effective practice in offender supervision. It also explores the potential of new methods of risk and needs assessment in the planning and evaluation of that supervision.

Further reading

By far the best account of the politicization of the problem of crime can be found in Downes and Morgan (1997). However, for an interesting perspective and analysis of this process in America, see Beckett (1997). The fullest account (and a very accessible explanation) of the crisis in the penal system at the end of the twentieth century is provided by Cavadino and Dignan (1997).

Notes

1 The murder of Jamie Bulger and the subsequent trial of the two young boys who killed him, for example, created a sharp dichotomy of view about whether they should be punished or treated.
2 This is what some people term the 'tariff', comprised of discharges, fines, community sentences and prison.
3 It is now an official objective under the regime of the new Director of Prisons, Martin Neary.
4 'Bifurcation' is shorthand for a sentencing policy of short sentences for relatively minor offenders, and long ones for the dangerous. Such a policy has obvious problems of definition: for instance, the answer to the question 'who is dangerous?' currently appears to be street robbers but not drink-drivers or owners of unsafe working environments.

chapter six

More punishment or more effectiveness? How some things work

The previous two chapters have explored how the probation service in England and Wales found itself under pressure during the 1980s and 1990s from a political climate which, until the change of government in 1997, had become progressively more punitive, populist and anti-welfare in its approach to offenders. Much of the impact of this was negative, and during the mid-1990s the probation service also experienced substantial cuts in its funding which increased workloads and added to the difficulties staff found in meeting more rigorous performance standards. However, other aspects of official policy during the same period were preparing the ground for a new role for probation, and trying to maintain some of the positive agenda which had been briefly established by the 1991 Criminal Justice Act's attempts to put probation 'centre stage' in the criminal justice system. For example, an inspection of the probation service's work with dangerous offenders (Her Majesty's Inspectorate of Probation 1995) identified many weaknesses in practice but was influential in outlining a new role for the service in public protection and risk management. At the same time as politicians and the public were rediscovering a taste for punishment, a new wave of research on the effectiveness of supervision was starting to show that the right kind of rehabilitative effort, applied to the right people, could make a contribution to reducing offending, which was one goal the rehabilitative agenda had in common with the popular agenda. This chapter describes the sources and strength of this new evidence, and begins to explore how it laid the basis for a new expectation that probation services could become crime-reduction services. As this and the next chapter show, this shift in expectations of probation became a central part of the evidence-based Crime Reduction Programme which was launched by the New Labour government elected in 1997, and a re-engineered probation service attracted considerable new resources for new tasks.

The rebirth of rehabilitation

Although the most famous exponent of 'nothing works', Robert Martinson, came from the United States, his views, as we saw in Chapter 4, were never universally accepted there. Indeed, the study on which his original paper was based had itself reached more measured and qualified conclusions, including some moderately positive findings about some projects. For example, both casework and counselling were found to have produced some positive results with offenders in some circumstances, even though their overall impact was small:

> to the degree that casework and individual counselling provided to offenders in the community is directed towards their immediate problems, it may be associated with reduction in recidivism rates. Unless this counselling leads to solution of problems such as housing, finances, jobs or illness which have high priority for offenders, it is unlikely to have any impact upon future criminal behaviour.
>
> (Lipton *et al.* 1975: 572)

Ironically the 'nothing works' doctrine was more dominant in Britain, where the mainly negative results of the IMPACT study had discouraged further government-sponsored research on the possible rehabilitative effects of probation. One consequence of this was that practitioners had to find their own sources of optimism and belief in what they were doing, and the 'nothing works' era actually became a period of creativity and enthusiasm in the development of new methods and approaches. These were often not evaluated and depended on the enthusiasm of a few officers, but within this pluralistic approach to practice can be found the forerunners of modern evidence-based approaches (Vanstone 2000). For example, the first attempts in Britain to introduce principles based on learning theory into mainstream probation practice came about through the work of two psychologists, James McGuire and Philip Priestley, who were to play a major role in the development of evidence-based practice. During the mid-1970s they offered courses to probation officers on methods published in a handbook of 'social skills and personal problem solving' (Priestley *et al.* 1978), and were also involved in the implementation of the methods in probation day centres and prisons. The methods used were based on 'life skills' and problem-solving techniques which were increasingly being taught by clinical psychologists to their patients or clients, and many of them were already in use in a Canadian project for unemployed young people called Saskatchewan Newstart. Later, when evaluation of the work in prisons indicated little effect on subsequent offending except among violent offenders, Priestley and McGuire developed and taught an approach based more specifically on the analysis and modification of offending behaviour (Priestley *et al.* 1984; McGuire and Priestley 1985).

Other early attempts to develop evidence-based practice in Britain can be found in such relatively neglected studies as Sinclair's (1971) attempt to account for differences between successful and unsuccessful probation hostels (the key factor turned out to be good hostel wardens, who combined warmth and concern with clarity about rules and expectations). Another study demonstrating the positive impact of pre-release work with prisoners (Shaw 1974) prefigured current concerns about the 'resettlement' of prisoners. However, official encouragement was lacking and, as described in Chapter 4, probation services in the 1980s were mainly seen as providing alternatives to custody. A brief official flirtation with emerging ideas about effective rehabilitation occurred during the preparation of the 1991 Criminal Justice Act, but the ensuing backlash and the adoption of a populist stance by new ministers in the mid-1990s led to an emphasis on punishment and incapacitation rather than rehabilitation. Strong government endorsement of an evidence-based rehabilitative approach had to await the election of a new Labour government in 1997. By then, significant strands of evidence had emerged in Britain and elsewhere to support the methods and techniques of a new model of rehabilitation.

The research behind the new rehabilitation

Summarizing research in a limited space always carries the risk of simplifying, and of omitting important caveats and reservations. However, it seems useful at this point to indicate what have been the main research influences on the current developments in community sentencing which have come to be known as 'What Works', if only in order to encourage readers to go and look at the research for themselves. Some of these studies have already been mentioned briefly in Chapter 4 as examples of the continuation of some research on effectiveness even during the 'nothing works' era, and other summaries are available, for example in Home Office publications issued to support the probation service's development strategy (Chapman and Hough 1998; McGuire 2000). Basically those studies which have influenced developments in the UK, and in some cases throughout the English-speaking world, fall into three groups, all of which produced significant output during the late 1980s and 1990s.

Cognitive-behavioural approaches

The first group of approaches to rehabilitation comprises the work of psychological criminologists, many of them Canadian, who have empha-sized the role of social learning and of thinking or cognition in the develop-ment and maintenance of offending. A feature of the environment in which this work has developed is that a number of key individuals have combined significant academic or research contributions with experience as prac-titioners within the criminal justice system, in a way which has always proved difficult in Britain (examples are Don Andrews, Jim Bonta, Paul Gendreau, Frank Porporino and Robert Ross). A clear statement of a social learning approach to offending is provided by, among others, Andrews and Bonta (1998) who set out an integrated theory of offending which connects social disadvantage, personality traits, thinking styles and social strategies into a model of how offending occurs and continues. For example, adverse social factors such as poverty and lack of opportunities can make it difficult for parents to provide a consistent and supportive environment for children. Personality characteristics such as impulsiveness or risk-seeking, perhaps reinforced by peer expectations, are likely to limit the benefits gained from formal education, while exposure to illegitimate opportunities and positive peer support for delinquency will make offending an attractive option. Add to this poor social skills and problem-solving abilities, perhaps due to rigid thinking, lack of awareness of alternatives and difficulty in appreciating or taking into account the views and needs of others, and offending becomes likely; add a strong possibility of getting away with the offence, or alterna-tively a penal response which stigmatizes and excludes without addressing any of these problems, and continued offending becomes more likely. Some of these 'risk factors' are 'static', meaning they have already happened and cannot now be changed (for example, a pattern of offending in the past) while others are, at least in principle, 'dynamic' or potentially subject to change (such as current attitudes, beliefs, behaviour and opportunities).

This kind of model also suggests a process of intervention based on chang-ing risk factors which are accessible and likely to make a difference: for example, habits of thinking ('cognition') and patterns of behaviour which can be changed to bring about better results for the individual. The process of change is often seen primarily as the acquisition of new skills. Such approaches are also consistent with the style of work advocated by McGuire and Priestley in Britain, but a particularly influential development in Canada and elsewhere was the idea of a 'programme' which put together a series of planned and sequential learning opportunities into a cumulative sequence, covering an appropriate curriculum of skills and allowing plenty of opportunity to reinforce learning through structured practice (often overlooked by UK practitioners of 'social skills' approaches in probation – see Hudson 1988). Robert Ross, for example, after carrying out research which identified a focus on thinking as a common feature of many successful interventions with offenders (Ross and Fabiano 1985), developed a programme called 'Reasoning and Rehabilitation' which systematically adopted a cognitive-behavioural focus (Ross et al. 1986) and was to exercise a widespread influence on work with offenders both in prisons and in the community. The influence of this programme is further discussed later in this chapter.

Research reviews and meta-analysis

The second major strand of research which helped to revive rehabilitation as a feasible goal in criminal justice was a series of research reviews which tried to pull together the findings of what was by now a substantial body of research in order to draw out general lessons about what approaches were likely to be effective. Some of these were carried out at the request of governments and were traditional narrative reviews which summarized a number of studies and pointed to shared or important findings: for example, McLaren (1992) in New Zealand and McIvor (1990) in Scotland. The latter was a particularly impressive piece of work and was destined to have a significant influence on developments throughout Britain. In general, the narrative research reviews of this period found more studies with positive outcomes than had been available to earlier reviewers such as Lipton et al. (1975).

In addition to this traditional style of review, researchers and practitioners were also beginning to benefit from the new statistical technique of meta-analysis which combines the results from a number of studies by coding them to a common framework and applying a common measure of 'effect size', that is, the extent to which outcomes for 'treated' groups differ from those for control groups or (in some studies) matched comparison groups. These methods have been criticized (e.g. by Mair 1995): coding a range of rather different studies to a common framework can introduce some distortions, and since not all studies record the same variables, some findings may in reality be based on fairly small numbers because few studies have looked at them, even though thousands of cases may be covered by the meta-analysis as a whole. Equally, the evidence base for the meta-analysis will reflect the subjects available for the original research, and we need to avoid over-confidence in drawing conclusions about adults from meta-analyses in which most of the studies have involved juveniles, or conclusions about female or ethnic minority populations from groups of studies which are mainly about white males. Different meta-analyses apply different selection criteria, different search techniques and sometimes slightly different standards of methodological rigour in choosing what studies to include, and there are also at least three different ways of calculating an effect size in use in current literature. However, there seems little room for doubt that meta-analysis has greatly increased our capacity to draw general conclusions by aggregating findings from a number of smaller studies, some of which might carry little weight on their own. Two major meta-analyses in particular have had a large influence on our current understanding of effective practice with offenders, one carried out in Canada (Andrews *et al.* 1990) which famously launched the principles of risk, need and responsivity (explained further below) and one in the United States (Lipsey 1992). Others (such as Izzo and Ross 1990) have made significant contributions, while some researchers have also begun to address the problems of groups which are under-represented in the research (e.g. Dowden and Andrews 1999).

Research on high-risk offenders

The third major strand of research which prepared the way for the 'What Works' movement of the 1990s was a small group of studies which provided reasonably convincing evidence for reductions in reconviction among fairly high-risk probationers who had, as part of their probation orders, participated in structured programmes of various kinds designed to address their offending. Such studies were a rarity in Britain after a decade of discouragement, but a few researchers had not completely accepted the 'nothing works' agenda and had the opportunity to carry out evaluative studies with local probation services. Two studies which showed positive results were published in the late 1980s. The first of these (Raynor 1988), carried out in South Wales, showed a group of young adult male probationers achieving a reconviction rate some 13 per cent below comparable offenders sentenced to custody, as well as reporting a reduction in social and personal problems. There was also evidence that the project had reduced the use of custodial sentences by local courts. The second study (Roberts 1989), carried out in Hereford and Worcester, also showed substantial reductions in offending by young adult probationers, including reductions not only in the number offending but also in the frequency of offending by those who did offend. Studies like these began to be noticed as probation managers and practitioners looked for positive content to introduce into the more rigorous and demanding forms of supervision envisaged by the government policy papers which led up to the 1991 Criminal Justice Act (Home Office 1988, 1990a).

Around the same time, those who actually looked at research from other countries (not a widespread habit in British probation at the time) could study the first comparative evaluation of the Reasoning and Rehabilitation programme (Ross *et al.* 1988) which showed particularly encouraging results. Other research such as the evaluations of American experiments with 'intensive supervision' also contained lessons for those who were interested in effectiveness (e.g. Petersilia 1990), although the overall results were less encouraging.

General lessons

The message of these various strands of research was encouraging: far from nothing working, it appeared that appropriate forms of supervision were capable of delivering reductions in offending of between 10 and 20 per cent, or even more in some cases.[1] Conversely, the wrong kind of supervision could do harm. Taken together, the research pointed to a number of characteristics of effective supervision which are listed in slightly different ways by different authorities but cover the same ground, and can be summarized as follows. In the present state of our knowledge, it appears likely that the more effective programmes are those which:

(i)   target high-risk offenders who are otherwise likely to continue to offend, rather than low-risk offenders who may gain little benefit or be harmed. This is Andrews's 'risk principle', nowadays usually interpreted as guidance to target a medium to high range, as the very highest-risk offenders are likely to be unresponsive except perhaps to very high levels of intervention, beyond what one programme is likely to provide. 'Risk' here refers to likelihood of reconviction rather than to dangerousness.

(ii)   focus on criminogenic need, that is, those characteristics or circumstances of offenders which have contributed to their offending (equivalent to 'dynamic risk factors'). This is Andrews's 'need principle'.

(iii) are highly structured, making clear and explicit demands and following a logical sequence determined by their learning goals.

(iv)   use a directive working approach, so that participants know what they are meant to be doing.

(v)   use broadly cognitive-behavioural methods, to provide opportunities to learn new thinking and behaviour. This kind of multi-modal, skills-oriented focus is likely to offer a learning style accessible to many offenders, and therefore to help to satisfy Andrews's 'responsivity principle' that programmes must promote the engagement and involvement of offenders by using an appropriate learning style and delivery.

(vi)   are best located in the community (though this does not mean they are ineffective in prison).
(vii)   have programme integrity, that is, are delivered as intended, with procedures to ensure this (for further explanation, see Hollin 1995).
(viii) have committed and effective management.
(ix)   have appropriately trained staff who believe they can be effective.
(x)   have adequate resources for continuity.
(xi)   have integral evaluation and feedback, ideally involving external researchers.

The emergence of programmes for probationers

The STOP programme

The first fully evaluated attempt in England and Wales to apply these principles to a programme for offenders supervised by the probation service was started in the (then) Mid Glamorgan Probation Service in South Wales in 1990, and known as Straight Thinking On Probation or STOP, a version of Ross's Reasoning and Rehabilitation programme. Ross's programme included modules on problem-solving, social skills, management of emotions, negotiation skills, critical reasoning, creative thinking and values enhancement. In Mid Glamorgan these were delivered over 35 two-hour sessions. Both the authors of this book were heavily involved from 1990 to 1997 in various aspects of the planning, implementation and evaluation of this project, and in the publication of its results (see, for example, Raynor and Vanstone 1994b, 1996, 1997; Raynor 1998). The evaluation study's findings concerning the programme's impact on offenders have been widely discussed in Britain, largely because of the shortage of other comparable studies. As a result, the STOP findings have been widely quoted as lending substantial support for cognitive-behavioural methods of supervision, and their impact may even appear disproportionate for what are in reality fairly modest results from a local study carried out with little research funding and, at the beginning, very little official encouragement at national level.

Readers interested in the full details of the study's methodology and findings may wish to refer to the more comprehensive account given in Raynor and Vanstone (1997). In brief, we were able to compare actual reconviction at 12 and 24 months for the STOP programme and for a number of comparison groups of male offenders with predicted reconviction rates based on static risk factors such as age and criminal record, using the best British prediction instrument available at that time (Home Office 1993). On this measure, several community sentences performed quite well with less serious offenders, but the nearest equivalent to the STOP group in terms of seriousness and persistence of offending was a comparison group of offenders receiving custodial sentences. The results of this comparison are set out in

Table 1: during comparable periods at risk (i.e. from date of probation order or release from custody respectively) the STOP programme completers were reconvicted less. During the first 12 months, they also reconvicted at well below the predicted rate, but during the second year of follow-up they caught up with the predicted rate, though still remaining below the custodial comparison group.

Several warning notes should be sounded here. First, as is common in local evaluation studies using fairly small numbers, few of these differences satisfy conventional tests of significance (the exception is a comparison between STOP completers and people released from young offender institutions; other comparisons of the STOP group with custodially sentenced offenders approach significance). Secondly, the results are nowhere near as dramatic as some of those reported for comparable programmes in Canada (Ross *et al.* 1988). On the other hand, we also found that Mid Glamorgan was in general a high-reconviction area, so that predictors based on national outcomes could under-predict for all the groups of offenders in our study. Also, given the relatively poor performance of non-completers, it is important to note that the completion rate was, for this type of programme, quite high at 75 per cent of those eligible to complete. This was broadly similar to completion rates for other community sentences at the time, but clearly

Table 1   Predicted and actual reconviction rates adjusted to eliminate pseudo-reconvictions ($N = 655$, sentenced during the first 10 months of the experiment)

	By 12 months		By 24 months	
	Predicted (%)	*Actual (%)*	*Predicted (%)*	*Actual (%)*
Started probation with STOP ($n = 107$)	44	44	63	65
Other probation ($n = 100$)	41	40	59	61
Community service ($n = 194$)	35	32	52	49
Suspended imprisonment ($n = 90$)	26	27	41	41
Imprisonment (adults < 12 mths) ($n = 82$)	38	44	55	56
Young offender institutions ($n = 82$)	47	54	65	73
Combined custodials ($n = 164$)	42	49	60	65
STOP completers ($n = 59$)	42	35	61	63

Source: Raynor and Vanstone (1997)

pointed to the maintenance and improvement of completion rates as a key component of future effectiveness. (The low completion rates achieved in some more recent programmes underline this message.)

What was rather more striking, in the case of the STOP programme completers, was a study of the seriousness of reconvictions and the sentences received on reconviction. Table 2 shows proportions of offenders reoffending seriously (defined as violent or sexual offences or burglary) and proportions receiving custodial sentences on reconviction, which can be taken as one measure of the seriousness of reconvictions at least as perceived by sentencers. Here the differences in favour of the STOP completers are more marked, particularly the low incidence of custodial sentences on reconviction (which resembles one of the findings of Ross et al. 1988).

In earlier reports of these findings we speculated that this might indicate that some STOP group members were changing their behaviour away from offences which had an obvious personal victim, rather than away from offending in general. Offences such as criminal damage or possession of drugs continued. Some support for this interpretation comes from the post-programme interviews, in which many programme members described ways in which they believed their thinking had changed: Table 3 shows the common themes in these interviews, which clustered particularly around becoming less impulsive and thinking more about other people's feelings and points of view. Several of the interviews illustrated this particularly clearly, for example:

> It's made me realize . . . it's learnt me to put myself in other people's places if they'd been burgled . . . guilty's the word . . . it's out of order.

> I sit down and work things out whereas before I'd just drink. I sit down

Table 2 Serious offences and custodial sentences on reconviction

	Serious offences on original conviction	Serious offences on reconviction at:		Custodial sentences on reconviction
		12 months	24 months	
Sentenced to STOP (n = 107)	42 (39%)	19 (18%)	29 (27%)	21 (20%)
Combined custodials (n = 164)	67 (41%)	34 (21%)	41 (25%)	25 (15%)
STOP completers (n = 59)	21 (36%)	5 (8%)	13 (22%)	1 (2%)

Source: Raynor and Vanstone (1997)

and look at my options and work it out that way instead of rushing off and doing something stupid.

Some other aspects of the study contributed to this general picture. Questionnaires designed to measure the extent of attitudes and beliefs favourable to crime and the level of self-reported social and personal problems (the CRIME-PICS instrument: Frude *et al.* 1990) were administered before and after the programme, and to comparison groups of offenders on 'standard' probation orders or community service (Table 4). Both the STOP programme and 'standard' probation appeared to have a positive effect on attitudes, and the STOP programme in particular was associated with a marked reduction in self-reported problems. This reduction was associated with lower reconviction rates ($p < 0.05$).

Table 3 Self-reported changes in thinking among programme participants

	No.	*(%)*
Thinking before acting, speaking or offending	16	28
Thinking a problem through	15	26
Thinking of consequences	14	24
Talking and explaining to people	10	17
Thinking of others	8	14
Thinking about who can help/involving others	6	10
Prioritizing/sorting out options	4	7
Understanding and/or listening to other viewpoints	4	7
Thinking positively	3	5
Dealing with a problem immediately	3	5
Thinking more clearly	2	3
More open and assertive	2	3
Less aggressive	2	3

Source: Raynor and Vanstone (1997)

Table 4 Changes in CRIME-PICS scores and reconvictions within 12 months

Component and direction of change	*Proportion (%) reconvicted*
Attitudes and beliefs become more pro-criminal ($n = 40$)	38
Attitudes and beliefs become more pro-social ($n = 55$)	27
Self-reported problems increase ($n = 31$)	48
Self-reported problems decrease ($n = 45$)	22

Source: Raynor and Vanstone (1997)

Overall, a fair summary of our findings in relation to the STOP programme's impact on its members would be that we found some evidence of fairly short-term reductions in offending and rather more persistent reductions in more serious offending among those who completed the programme. These were associated with reported changes in attitudes, thinking and behaviour consistent with the rationale of a cognitive-behavioural programme, and offered a more effective and constructive sentencing option than other likely sentences for this group of relatively serious and persistent offenders. However, the findings also pointed to a need to improve the matching of offenders to the programme and the proportion completing it: some programme members were clearly selected on a tariff basis, being at high risk of a custodial sentence, rather than on the basis of assessed needs appropriate to the programme. Most importantly, our findings pointed to a need to reinforce what was learned during the programme by appropriate follow-up during the remainder of the period of supervision.

Pathfinder programmes, accreditation and the National Probation Service

While this and other local experiments were proceeding, managers, practitioners and researchers who were interested in the practical implications of new ideas about effective practice were organizing an annual series of 'What Works' conferences to disseminate the new ideas (a number of papers from the first three of these were eventually published; see McGuire 1995). A conference organized by Colin Roberts at Green College, Oxford, also helped to promote the new approaches, and in 1993 the Home Office organized a conference in Bath, followed by another conference in London in 1995 on 'Managing What Works'. This was followed by a circular encouraging (or requiring) probation services to adopt effective methods and promising follow-up action by the independent Probation Inspectorate (although, as many pointed out at the time, the relevant evidence base for Britain was at that stage quite small).

Involvement of the Inspectorate, and of the then Chief Inspector Graham Smith (later Sir Graham), proved to be an essential catalyst in taking forward the 'What Works' agenda (or, as it was known then, the Effective Practice Initiative). Instead of a simple inspection, a research exercise was set up involving a detailed survey of probation areas by Andrew Underdown, a senior probation manager who was already closely involved in issues around effective practice. The results (Underdown 1998) were an eye-opener: of the 267 programmes which probation areas claimed they were running based on effective practice principles, evidence of effectiveness based on reasonably convincing evaluation was available only for four (one of which was not actually included in the responses to the initial survey). One of these was the Mid Glamorgan STOP programme (Raynor and Vanstone 1997); the others were in London, where John Wilkinson played an important role in programme evaluation (Wilkinson 1998).

These very poor results pointed to the need for a centrally managed initiative to introduce more effective forms of supervision, and the election in 1997 of a new government committed to evidence-based public policy created a climate in which political support could be gained for such an initiative. The Home Office's Probation Unit worked closely with the Inspectorate to develop what was now the What Works initiative; good publications were issued to promote awareness (Chapman and Hough 1998; McGuire 2000) and a number of promising programmes were identified for piloting and evaluation as 'Pathfinder' programmes, with support in due course from the Government's Crime Reduction Programme. The Pathfinder project included several cognitive-behavioural programmes (one of them designed by James McGuire, and another being a revised version of Reasoning and Rehabilitation) but also included work on basic skills (improving literacy and numeracy to improve chances of employment), pro-social approaches to supervision in community service, and a number of joint projects run by probation services with prisons and in some cases voluntary organizations, working on the resettlement of short-term prisoners after release. Evaluations of the Pathfinder programmes are incomplete at the time of writing, but some encouraging interim findings are beginning to emerge (e.g. Hatcher and McGuire 2001).

In the meantime a new probation service was taking shape, to come formally into existence as a National Probation Service in April 2001, replacing the old separate area probation services and explicitly committed to public protection and crime reduction. The roll-out of accredited programmes was continued well beyond the original Pathfinder pilots, with a very ambitious training programme and a new management structure involving programme managers and treatment managers to ensure the implementation and integrity of the 'What Works' initiatives. In particular, much was learned from developments in the prison service which, although starting later than the probation service, had put in place a well-managed and well-monitored range of cognitive-behavioural programmes aimed originally at the treatment of sex offenders, and later expanded to include general offending programmes (including Reasoning and Rehabilitation). A particular feature of the prison programmes was rigorous and continuing evaluation (see, for example, Beech et al. 1998; Friendship et al. 2001).

While probation services were struggling with a variety of unevaluated local initiatives, the prison service had developed a quality assurance system based on an accreditation panel with international expert membership to ensure that only programmes with a convincing evidence base were used, and on a comprehensive audit system to inspect the delivery of programmes and ensure integrity. Many hundreds of offenders had passed through programmes supported by this system. After some debate, the Home Office decided to adopt similar systems to support the emerging curriculum of pro-grammes in the probation service and a Joint Prison/Probation Accredit-ation Panel was formed in 1999, with a number of new members and the inclusion of experts on probation matters (Joint Prison/Probation Accredit-ation Panel 2000). From being unable in 1997 to point to more than a hand-ful of evaluated effective initiatives, the probation service had been transformed within a few years into an organization able to offer quality-controlled programmes throughout England and Wales, in what is believed to be the largest initiative in evidence-based corrections to be undertaken anywhere in the world.

Risks, needs and effective case management

Our brief account of the STOP evaluation has already indicated how ques-tions of assessment, targeting and overall case management were beginning to be seen as important. If offenders were to be influenced, this would be the outcome of the whole period of supervision, of which the programme was a part, rather than simply of the programme itself. Also, attention was needed to the practical difficulties and social stresses faced by offenders during supervision: often these were not addressed by programmes themselves, which concentrated on teaching problem-solving skills for long-term benefit rather than on assistance with immediate problems. Nevertheless, offenders overwhelmed by difficulties of coping and survival in the community were less likely to attend and complete their programmes; others needed targeted attention to problems such as substance abuse which limited their ability to benefit from other opportunities. In prisons programmes could be delivered within a fairly stable but understimulating environment, and attendance and completion rates were good; programmes in the community faced more obstacles and more competition for the offender's attention.

All this pointed to the need for a thought-out case management process based on careful assessment of risks and needs. Case management is still the subject of basic research to identify possible models, but it is clear that com-pletion rates for community-based programmes vary from area to area and are often very low: although the Jersey Probation Service achieved 100 per cent completion in a Reasoning and Rehabilitation programme in 1999, this is quite exceptional and mainland probation areas are nowhere near achiev-ing this, often having only a minority of starters actually completing. The original STOP completion rate looks good by current standards, and much remains to be done to bring case management up to the level of efficacy which now seems achievable in programmes. However, where a good deal of learning has taken place during the 1990s is on the subject of risk assess-ment.

Probation services in England and Wales have only recently begun to use standardized instruments for the assessment of 'risk' and 'need'. Less than a decade ago this practice was almost unknown in the United Kingdom, and its recent growth has been associated particularly with the use of the two instruments which were the focus of a recent Home Office study (Raynor *et al.* 2000) – the Level of Service Inventory – Revised (LSI-R) developed in Canada (Andrews and Bonta 1995), and the Assessment, Case Management and Evaluation instrument (ACE) developed by the Probation Studies Unit in England (Roberts *et al.* 1996). The underlying principles are now so widely accepted that the Home Office is developing a comprehensive assessment instrument intended for use in all prisons and probation services (OASys Project Team 1999) to underpin the wider 'What Works' initiative (Home Office 1999).

The requirement that probation officers should routinely undertake assessments of the 'risk' presented by the offenders with whom they came into contact was first embodied in the National Standards issued in 1992 and repeated with greater emphasis when the Standards were revised in 1995 (Home Office 1992, 1995a). However, there were no widely accepted methods of doing this other than relying on the judgement of individual probation officers. Public protection was increasingly seen as a core task of the probation service, particularly as all prisoners serving medium or long sentences were now subject to supervision on release under the provisions of the 1991 Criminal Justice Act. No doubt the probation service was to some extent reflecting the wider preoccupation with 'risk' which social scientists (e.g. Beck 1992) were identifying as a particular feature of late modern societies, but the service also had concrete and specific reasons of its own to be concerned about risk as its role in the criminal justice system changed. An inspection of work with potentially dangerous offenders led to considerable concern about how consistently risk assessment was carried out in such cases (Her Majesty's Inspectorate of Probation 1995) and a considerable amount of development and training activity began to be undertaken around issues of 'risk'.

Much of this activity initially concentrated on raising awareness of risk as an issue in probation services' management and practice, and on conceptual clarification (Kemshall 1996): for example, the term 'risk' is often used to mean both the probability of *any* reoffending, and the danger of a very harmful violent offence, where the issues of concern will often be the nature of the possible offence and which potential victims are threatened rather than simply the probability of an offence occurring within a given time. This kind of ambiguity about whether 'risk' primarily indicates the probability of further offences or the danger presented should they occur can lead to confusion, for example over what is meant by a 'high-risk' offender: is this someone very likely to commit further offences of a routine nature, or someone whose next offence is likely to be serious if it occurs? At the same time, Home Office researchers were developing another approach to risk, which was based on using information about offenders' criminal records to provide a quantified estimate of the probability of further offences within a given period (Copas 1992). This approach was regarded both as a contribution to risk assessment and as an aid to evaluative research, since it allowed researchers to calculate expected reconviction rates for groups of offenders subjected to particular sentences or forms of supervision and to compare these with the rates actually achieved (see, for example, Raynor and Vanstone 1994a; Lloyd *et al*. 1994). It eventually led to the development of a very effective 'static' predictor, the Offender Group Reconviction Scale.

Other developments in and around probation services in the 1990s also contributed to increasing interest in systematic assessment. Reference has already been made to the Canadian meta-analytic research (Andrews *et al*. 1990) which indicated that the most effective programmes were those which targeted higher- rather than lower-risk offenders; which addressed needs or problems which contributed to offending; and which achieved a match between programme style and content and the needs and learning styles of offenders (responsivity). These three principles of risk, need and responsivity were widely quoted and helped to generate awareness of a need for more systematic assessment of offenders' needs to inform programme content and supervision plans. Evaluation of some probation programmes tended to support the view that better matching of programmes to offenders' needs could help improve effectiveness. At the same time, the growing interest in effective and evidence-based probation practice led to an interest in methods of measuring the effectiveness of supervision through tests administered at the beginning and end of periods of supervision, rather than waiting typically two or three years for the completion of a reconviction study. This led some services to rely heavily on psychometric tests and psychological expertise to measure intermediate targets of supervision, that is, targets of change which were believed to contribute to lower offending (e.g. McGuire *et al*. 1995) while others were interested particularly in attitudes and problems associated with offending, and a new instrument, CRIME-PICS, was developed for this purpose (Frude *et al*. 1994). The Home Office itself supported research on a simple 'needs assessment' instrument (Aubrey and Hough 1997).

All these approaches had specific advantages and disadvantages which contributed to the practice climate in which ACE and LSI-R became widely adopted. For example, the development of reconviction predictors from a national database of criminal records along the lines initially indicated by Copas's research led eventually to the Offender Group Reconviction Scale (Home Office 1996) and subsequent revisions: these provide a powerful evaluative tool in reconviction studies and contribute to central monitoring of the effectiveness of criminal justice agencies, but cannot help practitioners assess needs or evaluate the impact of supervision, since they include no factors which supervision can alter (in other words, they are based on 'static' or historical characteristics of offenders, not on 'dynamic' factors such as criminogenic needs, which could change). The needs assessment scale evaluated by Aubrey and Hough seemed unreliable for measuring changes during supervision, while CRIME-PICS appeared to be a good measure for some intermediate targets of supervision and significantly related to reconviction, but not as strongly related as some other measures (Raynor 1998). However, a further Home Office study suggested that knowledge of social factors impacting on offenders might slightly improve the accuracy of reconviction predictors based solely on criminal records, which tended to strengthen the case for the inclusion of some dynamic factors in risk prediction (May 1999). In this context, it was not surprising that some probation services and probation researchers became increasingly interested in the concept of risk prediction based on the assessment of criminogenic needs, or 'risk/need assessment', as already practised in Canada and elsewhere.

Risk/need assessment: prospects and possibilities

Risk/need assessment has been described as a 'third generation' method of risk prediction (Bonta 1996), with the first generation represented by the individual judgement of practitioners and the second by actuarial methods based solely on static factors such as criminal history. In principle, a well-designed and well-tested risk/need assessment instrument which incorporates assessment of criminogenic needs into the calculation of a risk score should be able to predict reconviction at much better than chance levels, to help practitioners target those dynamic risk factors which, if changed, can contribute to a reduction in future offending, and to measure, through repeated administration, whether changes are occurring during supervision which are likely to affect future offending. The potential attractiveness of such approaches, in a probation service required to develop evidence-based practice, is readily apparent: however, there was no significant tradition in the UK of developing and working with such assessment methods. This meant that instruments for use in the UK would either need to be new designs requiring a relatively lengthy period of development and testing, or would need to be imported, and would still require re-evaluation and validation in the UK practice context.

In fact the evaluation of LSI-R and ACE in England and Wales (Raynor *et al.* 2000) produced a number of interesting findings which support the feasibility of the risk/needs approach and which are helping inform the development of the Home Office's own instrument. Both LSI-R and ACE predict reconviction at far better than chance levels, and LSI-R in particular performs almost as well as the latest version of the Home Office's Offender Group Reconviction Scale. Both also provide assessments of need and, most importantly, both are capable of functioning as 'risk-related change measures': in other words, their repeated administration can show changes in scores which are actually reflected in changes in the rate of reconviction. People whose risk/needs scores decrease during supervision have a lowered risk of reconviction compared to their starting point. Moreover, the use of such instruments for repeated assessments can help document the impact of supervision on the criminogenic needs of offenders, and helps to show what probation officers are achieving.

To sum up, the 1990s were a period of fundamental transformation in our understanding of how offenders could be supervised successfully in the community. Key components of an effective approach, which at the beginning of the decade were the focus of interest for only a few researchers and practitioners, were by its end part of an officially recognized and endorsed strategy, underpinned by some serious research (not yet enough) and prompting a considerable reorganization of the process of supervising offenders. These components included effective programmes, cognitive/behavioural approaches, accreditation, risk and need assessment, case management and a commitment to research. The next chapter attempts a brief appraisal of where we are now and what other developments may be needed.

Further reading

Readers interested in a full understanding of the background and history of 'What Works' can do no better than go to McGuire (1995). A full description of relevant research is provided by Goldblatt and Lewis (1998). For a very interesting recent critical analysis, see Robinson (2001) and Vanstone (2000).

Note

1 Caution is sometimes needed in interpreting the reports. For example, if 40 per cent of the experimental group reconvict compared to 50 per cent of the comparison group, some will (correctly) describe this as a 10 per cent difference, while others will (again correctly) report that the experimental group's reconviction rate was 20 per cent less, because 40 is 80 per cent of 50.

chapter seven

Community penalties today

An overview of current community sentences
Enforcement and breach
The government's aims for criminal justice
A new sentencing policy?
Community safety and community justice
Risk, justice and diversity
Reintegration and legitimacy
Rehabilitation and community interests
Learning from social work?
Further reading

After our long journey from missionary origins via social casework, alternatives to custody and 'What Works', where have we arrived? Any attempt to sum up the current state of community penalties is hazardous and temporary, since the situation changes month by month: over 130 probation circulars were issued in the first nine months of 2001, not far short of one every working day. However, it is possible to outline current responsibilities, together with an indication of what seems to be being achieved and what risks and obstacles may need to be addressed. Following the rule which we have broadly adopted throughout this book, our definition of community penalties (what some people characterize as punishment in the community) fits those definitions provided in the 1991 Criminal Justice Act and now incorporated, with subsequent amendments, in the Powers of Criminal Courts Act 2000 and the Criminal Justice and Court Services Act 2000. In other words, our definition encompasses primarily those sentences which can be imposed on adults and are supervised by the probation service, but extends also to community sentences designed for younger offenders and supervised normally by youth offending teams which are led by local authorities and involve probation staff as members.

An overview of current community sentences

The community sentences available at the time of writing for adults (aged 16 and over) are as follows:

1 Community rehabilitation orders (the former probation orders) which require an offender to keep in contact with the probation service and cooperate with arrangements made for his or her supervision, which can include participation in programmes. Other requirements can be included by the court, such as residential requirements, attendance at specified activities or a 'probation centre', treatment for mental illness or addictions, curfew or exclusion requirements and abstinence from drugs. These orders can be made for up to three years, though shorter periods are normal, and, like all community sentences, they are subject to enforcement proceedings if offenders do not comply with their requirements. This normally means that the probation service initiates a prosecution for breach of the order, which if proved can lead to various sentences but is often dealt with by imprisonment.

2 Community punishment orders (the former community service orders) which require an offender to perform, under probation service supervision (directly or indirectly through other organizations), a set number of hours of unpaid work for the benefit of the community. The required hours can range from 40 to 240.

3 Community punishment and rehabilitation orders (the former 'combination order', a less than transparent title) which combine the requirements of a community punishment order (up to 100 hours) with those of a community rehabilitation order.

4 Drug treatment and testing orders, which require offenders to undergo treatment in relation to drug problems, supported by regular tests to detect illicit drug use and reviewed at intervals by the court. These orders are normally managed on behalf of the probation service by specialist drug treatment agencies working in partnership with the service, and failure to comply or positive drug tests can lead to breach action. The orders are a recent innovation now being implemented throughout Great Britain after broadly encouraging findings from pilot projects (Turnbull *et al.* 2000).

5 One of the less used adult community sentences is the curfew order, requiring an offender to stay at a particular location between particular hours for 2–12 hours in any one day. The order cannot last more than six months and can be supported by electronic monitoring ('tagging') where local facilities exist (Whitfield 1997).

6 Also available for some offenders (aged 21 or over, and only if sentenced in the Crown Court) is the suspended sentence supervision order, something of a survival from earlier legislation which requires an offender to

be supervised during all or part of the period of suspension of a suspended prison sentence (these are usually suspended for two years).

Community sentences for juveniles include the long-established supervision order which places a young offender (aged from 10–18) under the supervision of (normally) a local authority for up to three years. Again a range of additional requirements is available and enforcement is possible in the event of breach, though this has never been the focus of so much attention here as it has in the case of adult offenders. More recently a number of new orders have been created, some of which are still being piloted and evaluated; not all of these are strictly 'community sentences' as described by the 1991 Act but they are similar in spirit, including: a reparation order requiring up to 24 hours of reparative activity to benefit the community or, with consent, the victim; a parenting order requiring the parents of offenders to attend parenting classes for three months, with the option of a further discretionary period; and an action plan order requiring a young offender to comply with a three-month action plan drawn up by an inter-agency team to address his or her difficulties.

There are also some widely used non-custodial penalties which are not classed as 'community sentences' although the offender remains in the community, because they lack the element of supervision. They are not normally referred to as 'punishment in the community' but are clearly punishments which people undergo outside penal establishments, and although any detailed discussion of them lies outside the scope of this book it is important to note that the proper use and development of community sentences depends on a sentencing strategy which also makes strategic use of other non-custodial sentences such as fines and discharges. The fine, in particular, is the most commonly used non-custodial sentence, and evidence suggests that it is quite effective, particularly for people who have not been in much trouble before. One study (Walker *et al.* 1981) found that for first offenders, the reconviction rate after a fine was about half that after a probation order. Any attempt to limit the use of community sentences for low-risk offenders (in line with 'What Works' principles) depends on having other more suitable non-custodial sentences available to impose on them, but in recent years the use of the fine has been declining. This may be partly due to sentencers' reluctance to impose fines on people already struggling with poverty; during the years of mass unemployment in the 1980s, many people appearing before courts were dependent on welfare benefits, often already with deductions to pay various bills and debts, and fining them did not seem a sensible option. Instead many were made subject to probation orders on 'welfare' grounds, which was a dubious use of probation resources and sometimes inappropriate in relation to the risks and needs actually presented.

The most promising attempt in recent years to increase the use of the fine was the 'unit fine' system introduced, after piloting, by the 1991 Criminal

Justice Act. This expressed the maximum fine for each offence as a number of units rather than a sum of money, and the value of a unit in a particular case was determined in the light of the offender's financial resources. This attempt to link fines systematically to ability to pay, and to move towards greater equality in the impact of penalties on offenders from different social groups, made fines easier to collect and reduced the need for enforcement. However, it was one of the first areas of the Act to fall into disfavour as sentencers rebelled against the expectation that they should punish the rich with the same degree of relative severity as they customarily used in punishing the poor. In spite of this history, the argument for extending the use of the fine by making it more equitable and easier to collect is still compelling, and the possibilities presented by a unit fine system surely deserve re-examination.

According to the most recent figures (National Probation Service 2001; Home Office 2001) the service is responsible for supervising well over 200,000 offenders at any one time, including about 61,000 on community rehabilitation orders, 46,000 on community punishment orders, 29,000 on community punishment and rehabilitation orders, and 7,000 on money payment supervision orders (which place a fined offender under supervision until the fine is paid). Another 80,000 are subject to statutory supervision on release from prisons and other custodial establishments, but only about 25,000 of these are actually being supervised in the community. All young offenders sentenced to custodial sentences and all adult prisoners sentenced to 12 months or more are subject to some form of supervision after release, for periods ranging from a few months following a short sentence to life following release from a life sentence. These forms of post-custodial supervision are not 'community sentences' but are increasingly seen as an integral part of a single sentence served partly in custody and partly in the community (Maguire and Raynor 1997), an idea which is developed further in the government's current review of sentencing policy (Halliday 2001).

Enforcement and breach

All these different forms of supervision, except for a very small amount of 'voluntary after-care' supervision (see Maguire et al. 2000), are underpinned by a process of enforcement, usually involving prosecution for failure to cooperate with supervision. This usually means failing to keep appointments without an acceptable reason. Until the 1990s such enforcement was largely a discretionary matter for supervising officers, some of whom made very little use of their enforcement powers. Politicians became convinced that enforcement needed to become more rigorous, both to increase the perceived credibility of community sentences as a disposal for those who would otherwise go to prison and to contribute to a shift in the public perception of probation away from its 'welfare' image towards a more explicit criminal justice role.

Successive editions of National Standards for the supervision of offenders (Home Office 1992, 1995a, 2000b) have progressively reduced discretion in this area and tightened requirements: the power to enforce has become a duty, and the second appointment missed without a valid reason now triggers breach action. The compliance of probation staff with these new requirements has increased dramatically through successive inspections (though still with considerable variation from area to area). More recently, discussion has begun to focus on some possible consequences of this approach. For example, the police may not give such a high priority to the enforcement of community sentences as probation officers are now obliged to, and this can cause delays in those cases where an arrest warrant has to be issued to secure the offender's appearance at court. (There have been reports of some American probation services maintaining their own armed arrest squads to get around this problem, but no British equivalents have been suggested yet.) Perhaps more important is the possible conflict between a rigid approach to breach and making the best use of programmes: average completion rates are currently low, and there is a need for an approach to enforcement which makes a positive contribution to motivating offenders to complete programmes rather than terminating orders and risking imprisonment for relatively minor instances of non-compliance (Ellis 2000). This is an argument not for ignoring breaches of requirements but for positive enforcement policies which reinforce compliance and promote completion of programmes of supervision. Again it seems possible that some new thinking on enforcement and discretion may emerge from the current sentencing review.

The government's aims for criminal justice

The published aims of the Home Office include the delivery of 'effective custodial and community sentences to reduce reoffending and protect the public'. In pursuit of this aim, the targets which have been announced for the new National Probation Service include increasing the number of offenders completing accredited programmes to 60,000 in 2004, which is intended to result in a 5 per cent reduction in reconvictions among those supervised by the service. This is part of, and consistent with, the ambitious Crime Reduction Programme launched in 1999 and concerned to develop effective practice in crime prevention and crime reduction throughout the criminal justice process (for a summary of the underpinning research, see Goldblatt and Lewis 1998). The attempt to develop more effective forms of supervision has included a strategy of piloting, evaluation and accreditation using an expert panel, as outlined in the previous chapter. At the time of writing, in addition to prison-based programmes, the panel has accredited or recognized (provisionally accredited) the following: four 'general offending' programmes including one designed for one-to-one delivery; two programmes for sex offenders; two substance misuse programmes; one programme for drink-impaired drivers; and one for aggressive offenders. Under active consideration are possible developments in community punishment orders based on pro-social approaches to supervision and the learning of basic skills, and approaches to the resettlement of short-term prisoners in the community based on positive case management and active linking to community resources.

Of course such processes have their critics: the reduction in the discretion of individual probation officers and the centrally driven nature of the 'What Works' programme (Robinson 2001) have generated understandable resistance, and the National Association of Probation Officers has debated motions condemning the whole 'What Works' initiative as reactionary and unproven. The Accreditation Panel has been attacked as allegedly dominated by North American psychologists with an exclusive commitment to cognitive-behavioural programmes (Mair 2000), but its actual composition is more diverse than this and it has accredited programmes using a range of methods both within and outside the cognitive-behavioural tradition, including therapeutic communities and 'twelve-step' programmes for substance misusers.

More telling, perhaps, are those critics who have argued (like Merrington and Stanley 2000) that the roll-out of accredited programmes has been running too far ahead of the evidence, and that central commitment to implementing the programmes has not waited for the results of the Pathfinder pilots. It is true that the evidence base in Britain is still fairly small, and although existing research projects will enable it to grow rapidly, not all of it will necessarily support the management decisions which have already been taken. Some of these may have to be changed if the commitment to evidence-based policy is to be maintained. On this question, the Accreditation Panel has consistently emphasized the provisional nature of all accreditation, the need for continuing evaluation, and the need to review accreditations that do not receive support from ongoing evaluation. However, it is also clear that such a position does not always appeal to managers and civil servants who would like more fixed knowledge and a clearer set of rules to guide policy, and will not find it easy to revisit and review basic elements of their strategy if new evidence points to a need to do so.

Evidence-based policy is a two-way street: future evidence may or may not support particular details of current policy, and not all our expectations about likely results will be fulfilled. Where we have evidence we should be guided by it, but where we do not we need to retain the flexibility to act on it as it emerges. However, it is also clear that launching major change in criminal justice services is a very political process and depends on recruiting political support at a time when resources are available. This requires a degree of opportunism to make the most of circumstances which may be very different and harder to influence by the time all the evidence is in.

A new sentencing policy?

One possibly far-reaching consequence of new understandings about 'what works' is the recent Halliday (2001) report which is intended as the first stage of a comprehensive review of sentencing policy and practice leading to new legislation and significant change. It is clear from the report that the emergence of effective programmes is leading some people to think about a more flexible sentencing framework, in which the implementation of a sentence could reflect the offender's participation in approved programmes or his or her response to them. This is related to the widely discussed possibility of a 'seamless sentence' for short-term prisoners, in which a period of custody will be combined with a period of supervised release but the precise point of release may depend on various individual characteristics or behaviour or response to 'treatment'.

According to the Home Office (2000a), the review was set up to 'identify and evaluate new, more flexible frameworks for sentence decision-making and sentence management, which join up custodial and community sentences'. There are several reasons why such flexible approaches to sentencing are beginning (again) to seem attractive, in addition to the restoration of some confidence in rehabilitative processes. The reasons include a penal environment in which, since 1992, much larger numbers of prisoners have been subject to compulsory post-release supervision and are in effect serving a mixed custodial and community-based sentence (Maguire and Raynor 1997); they may also include the disappointment of a generation of policy-makers and practitioners who hoped that the 'just deserts' framework embodied in the 1991 Criminal Justice Act would lead to long-term reductions in imprisonment. The review may even contain traces of the centuries-old argument between executive and judiciary about who controls criminal justice. However, those who remember the consequences of social workers' unfettered discretion in the heavily custodial juvenile justice system of the 1970s (Morris and Giller 1983), or the perceived inequity of many parole decisions prior to the Carlisle (Home Office 1988b) report, will be concerned (in our view rightly) at the prospect of offenders having their sentences extended in order to be required to undertake programmes from which they might or might not benefit, or indeed having their sentences effectively shortened in response to some official judgement of 'good progress', with all the potential for arbitrariness and discrimination that such processes involve.

Whatever balance eventually emerges between 'flexibility' and justice, one very likely consequence of the Halliday review is a new approach to short-term prisoners. This will end the current neglect of a group of needy and often risky offenders who receive little assistance in prison and virtually none to resettle more successfully in the community after release (Maguire *et al.* 2000). For this group, a new sentence is proposed consisting of a short period of custody followed by supervision in the community backed up by the threat of a return to prison in the event of failure to comply. One possibility under discussion is that for some offenders who currently receive short prison sentences there might be no custodial component and they could move straight to the 'supervision' phase. Whatever version of this is eventually embodied in legislation, it is clear that the prison and probation services will work more closely together in future, and that the boundary between custodial and community sentences is becoming more fluid. This tendency is already present in collaboration over arrangements for the statutory through care of prisoners (which increasingly involves responsibility for reinforcing the effect of programmes delivered in prison), and in the current pilot projects exploring the 'resettlement' of short-term prisoners.

Community safety and community justice

As well as collaborating more with prisons in a 'seamless' approach to sentence management, the probation service is increasingly involved with other agencies in the community in new forms of partnership to manage risky offenders and to promote community safety. Probation plays its part in local 'crime and disorder' partnerships which have been set up in all local authority areas under the 1998 Crime and Disorder Act; these develop joint strategies to address local crime problems by involving not only criminal justice agencies but also providers of social resources such as housing, education and social services departments. Some of the same agencies are typically brought together with probation and police services in 'public protection panels' to manage identified groups of high-risk or dangerous offenders by collaborating over their surveillance and sharing information about risky behaviour so that preventative measures or enforcement action can be taken (Kemshall and Maguire 2001). These new patterns of work pose interesting challenges for probation staff and managers collaborating with other agencies which traditionally have different preoccupations and concerns, but they fit well with the new emphasis on public protection as a core function of the probation service. A similar shift in focus is involved in the service's recently acquired responsibilities towards victims of crime, which can include consultation about the discretionary release of prisoners responsible for their victimization (Williams 1999).

Developments such as these open up yet more new ways of thinking about the possible roles and functions of probation. For example, in the

United States, where 'community safety' is widely seen as the main goal of criminal justice agencies, some probation managers and practitioners have campaigned for the 'reinvention' of probation as a community safety agency working with others to impact on local crime and disorder problems. They advocate a 'broken windows' model of probation (Reinventing Probation Council 2000), drawing on the arguments of those American criminologists who point out how early signs of disorder and neglect in a neighbourhood can prepare the way for more and more serious crimes, creating a spiral of social decline (e.g. Wilson and Kelling 1982). The vision is of an accountable probation service serving the community by achieving crime reduction targets in collaboration with other agencies. This is advanced as an alternative to an outmoded model of probation as social work, which in many communities no longer attracts significant support or resources. Such arguments might at first sight seem like a subordination of probation's distinctive role to the task of assisting other agencies in their law enforcement functions. However, a more positive vision is suggested by research in Vermont, according to which what the public expects from criminal justice agencies, and by implication from community sentencing, can be summed up as:

- Safety from violent predators;
- Accountability for the offense;
- Repair of the damage done;
- Education and treatment of the offender; and
- Involvement in making decisions.

(Reinventing Probation Council 2000: 10)

They also advocate the active involvement of probation officers in community problems and in communication with citizens about them, outside their offices and if necessary outside office hours. Overall, many of their proposals are not far distant from some of the ideas explored in this book, and despite being expressed in the politicized language of American communitarianism they nevertheless help to point the way towards a community dimension for 'what works'.

Risk, justice and diversity

An important question raised by proposals of this kind and other risk-driven approaches to community safety is how far they can be pursued while attempting to adhere to accepted notions of justice and individual rights. As we indicated in the previous chapter, an effective risk/need assessment system is seen as an essential foundation for effective practice, since it offers the possibility of matching programmes or supervision to offenders' assessed needs and can also be used on a repeated basis to produce at least an approximate measurement of changes in risk during (or as a result of) supervision. However, serious concerns have also been expressed about the possible long-term impact of these new technologies of risk, not simply in terms of their contribution to a general preoccupation with risk in late modern society (Beck 1992) but also in relation to three specific issues. These concern the possible erosion of accepted standards of justice and civil rights; the possible misclassification of women offenders and of members of ethnic minorities; and the danger that because they identify adverse social and environmental factors as increasing the risk, they could lead to more severe punishment and coercive control for the poor simply because the poor already experience more disadvantages.

All of these criticisms raise serious concerns about justice. The first is particularly associated with the work of Feeley and Simon (1992), who point to the possibility of 'actuarial justice' in which the relative severity of penalties and level of surveillance or coercion is determined not by desert but by membership of groups with a low or high assessed risk of offending. Other critics have focused on the application to women and ethnic minorities of predictive instruments based primarily on research about white male offenders (Shaw and Hannah-Moffatt 2000). (The same point can be made about the research base of many programmes.) It is argued that this can lead to the overprediction of risk, the inclusion of irrelevant risk factors, or a failure to focus on significant needs of women or minorities which are less prevalent among white males. More generally, critical criminologists such as Hudson (1996) have argued that because indicators of risk include adverse social circumstances to which the poor are differentially exposed, the adoption of apparently 'scientific' and 'neutral' risk assessment methods can result simply in the increasing criminalization and incarceration of the disadvantaged. However, it is arguable that some of the research on risk/needs assessment offers some partial reassurance, or at least points the way to some possible safeguards.

For example, the recent evaluative work in probation services suggests that risk/need assessment techniques are actually being used to support rehabilitation. In other words, identification of a need as a risk factor can actually increase the chance that somebody does something to address the need, and that offenders' lives improve as a result, together with a real reduction in their average risk of reconviction (Raynor et al. 2000). Of course, this happens only with assessment instruments which include dynamic factors. The implication is that provided they are used as designed to support decisions about rehabilitative services, the risk of an unwitting disservice to offenders may be less. In a society which is generally hostile to offenders we may have to relabel their needs as risk factors in order to persuade policy-makers to take their needs seriously.

The argument that models of risk assessment based on white male majorities in offending populations can disadvantage women and ethnic minorities is the subject of lively debate (see, for example, Gelsthorpe 2001). Available studies show criminogenic needs or risk factors for women to be in some respects similar to, and in some respects different from those of men (Coulson *et al.* 1996; Dowden and Andrews 1999; Clark and Howden-Windell 2000). Where there seems to be broad agreement is that more research on 'What Works' issues for women offenders is needed, and the same is true for ethnic minorities, where there is general support for the idea of culturally appropriate ways of delivering rehabilitation but a limited amount of research to show how. There is also a limited amount of research which tends to support a degree of cross-cultural validity in well-designed assessment instruments (see, for example, Bonta 1993) but this tends to be concerned with broad predictive validity rather than with the fine detail of assessments.

What is also clear is that both female and ethnic minority offenders tend to experience patterns of disadvantage, discrimination or abuse which are likely to be different from those experienced by white male offenders, and are likely to be under-researched precisely because they affect a minority of the offending population available for research. This clearly runs the risk of reinforcing social injustice, and this is also evident when, for example, effective programmes in a probation area are based on groupwork with men and are denied to women because there are never enough of them to form a group. Current research on the needs of black and Asian probationers, together with the piloting of a variety of supervision models, should lead to some reduction of the problems recently identified by the Probation Inspectorate's thematic inspection of race equality issues in probation (Her Majesty's Inspectorate of Probation 2000).

It is not feasible for criminal justice policies or practices to try to correct general inequalities in society which require a much broader approach, and the risk assessment methods which correctly identify the greater social difficulties faced by people in poverty are not responsible for creating those difficulties. It is questionable whether we would prefer decisions to be made without knowing anything about the social difficulties offenders face, and the practice of sentencing the poor as if they had the same opportunities as the rich to lead crime-free lives has been rightly criticized, sometimes by the same commentators who express reservations about risk assessment (e.g. Hudson 1987). Risk/need assessment can open the way to effective help, not simply to graduated degrees of coercive control. However, it would be pointless to deny that the danger of 'actuarial justice' exists, and the possibility of basing sentences on likely future behaviour as well as past behaviour is one aspect of the new interest in 'flexible' sentencing.

Reintegration and legitimacy

'Community justice' and associated ideas such as restorative justice, reparation, relational justice and reintegrative shaming have been written about so
widely and so persuasively, particularly by active reformers such as Braithwaite (1989), that it would be absurd and inappropriate to attempt any kind
of comprehensive coverage here. Instead we try to draw out some considerations that seem to be particularly relevant to thinking about community
safety and community penalties. Restorative justice, in particular, seems to
be an international focus for creative and optimistic thinking: at the recent
United Nations Congress on the Prevention of Crime and the Treatment of
Offenders in Vienna, restorative justice was by far the most discussed
approach to sentencing, but the discussion centred more on its values and
social purposes than on its beneficial results, which were largely taken for
granted. To take just one example, the Friends World Committee for Consultation (2000) submitted a paper which argued that:

> The Quaker belief that there is intrinsic value in everyone calls for a
> vision of justice that maximizes the opportunities for transformation,
> forgiveness and reconciliation. Fundamental to these processes is heal-
> ing of the damage that is both cause and effect of crimes . . . We believe
> that through restorative processes we can build stronger communities
> and peaceful societies.

To take some other examples, Marshall's (1999) overview of restorative
justice research for the Home Office finds a good deal of evidence that
participants in restorative processes usually welcome them and often rate
them as more satisfactory than conventional criminal justice processes, but
finds as yet much less evidence of a reductive impact on future offending
(though some evidence of this is reported in Miers *et al.* 2001). The reasons
for advocating restorative justice approaches often seem to lie in their perceived moral appropriateness or presumed educative effects on participants,
but some other claimed advantages are less clear: for example, as Haines
(1998) pointedly asks, what exactly is restorative justice seeking to restore?

Some similar issues have arisen in respect of social reintegration in the current Home Office research on the 'resettlement' of short-term prisoners. The
term 'resettlement' has been devised to replace the old-fashioned terms
'through-care' and 'after-care', apparently in obedience to a political belief
that even if criminal justice services do care for offenders, this should not be
advertised too openly. However, for many short-term prisoners 'resettlement' seems an inappropriate term, as they were not very settled in the first
place: the aim can hardly be to restore them to a pre-sentence situation
which was deprived, criminogenic and generally disadvantageous. A more
appropriate strategy would be to seek to involve them in a new set of pro-
social linkages, resources and opportunities; this is certainly a strategy for

social integration or inclusion, but it is not *re*settlement or *re*integration. Instead it is intervention to try to bring about a new and more constructive state of affairs. This is perhaps a clue to the meaning of 'community' in the network of reintegrative ideas around 'community justice': 'community' is being used in its ideal and aspirational sense, as in the Friends' statement quoted above. 'Community justice' is connected with the struggle to develop and improve communities, and to promote a better quality of community living with more cooperation, more mutual aid and more collective problem-solving. It points to an improved standard of social conduct and pro-social opportunities, and it promotes forms of criminal justice practice which are seen as consistent with these.

Real communities, on the other hand, may be divided, hostile, stratified, prejudiced, exclusive, in active internal conflict or simply not characterized by any high level of social interaction between their supposed 'members'. They may be candidates for improvement, but the improvement is still in the future. As Zedner and Lacey's (1995) research on the idea of community in British and German criminal justice policy has shown, even within criminal justice discourse the same word can carry a very different set of associations and assumptions, depending on culture, history and tradition: some concepts of 'community' may be much less welcoming to perceived 'outsiders' than others. In many actual communities, justice under the control of the community is an unattractive option (the recent anti-paedophile riots in the UK have provided a graphic illustration of this). Instead, criminal justice processes perhaps need largely to remain under accountable professional control but also to act as a focus for communication with the 'community' or sections of it, with the aspiration that this may eventually lead to more appropriate community involvement in helping to handle the problems arising from crime. 'Community justice' involves a normative concept of community which is worth pursuing where possible for the sake of the values it represents, but whether restorative processes can really replace conventional criminal justice and move 'from margins to mainstream' (Restorative Justice Consortium 2000) seems to depend on the availability of a quality of community life which is far from universal.

Other formulations of a possible inclusive basis for criminal justice policy and practice have relied less on the questionable notion of 'community' and more on notions of interconnectedness or mutual concern. For example, Smith's (1998) discussion of socially inclusive approaches to social work with offenders points to the potential of 'peacemaking criminology' (Pepinsky and Quinney 1991) to inform the development of practical approaches to problem-solving and conflict resolution which encourage dialogue, involvement and connectedness, and seek to promote social solidarity and social justice. This is not an argument that 'community' necessarily already exemplifies these qualities, but that we should look for practical opportunities to promote them. In a similar vein, feminist commentators on criminal justice have pointed to different ways of doing justice: Heidensohn (1986) has written of 'Portia' and 'Persephone' models, the former representing an approach governed by formal rules and the latter guided more by situational thinking, needs, relationships and an ethic of care (see also Masters and Smith 1998). Daly (1989) has pointed out that both these approaches clearly exist even within the current male-oriented criminal justice system, and are not straightforwardly identifiable simply as male and female ways of thinking: perhaps the practical problem is how to influence the balance of these approaches, as well as ensuring that those who are presently ill served by criminal justice get a better deal. What these ideas have in common (put in a slightly different voice) is that they encourage pro-social approaches to resolving problems, drawing on positive forms of community involvement to do so.

Pro-social orientations, processes and outcomes can be expected to reinforce pro-social learning and lead to more of the same. The promotion of pro-social attitudes and behaviour through modelling and through reinforcing pro-social attitudes and responses is now recognized as an aspect of effective supervision, supported by research (e.g. Trotter 1993) and training. Some influential advocates of these approaches have linked them explicitly to questions of legitimacy, on the grounds that people are more likely to comply with the expectations of institutions and processes they see as fair, as respecting their rights, and as having the right to make demands on them (see, for example, Rex and Matravers 1998). While the research base for this idea is still small, at least within criminal justice, the arguments are quite persuasive and offer a possible way forward to address the supposed 'loss of confidence' in probation services by politicians and the public. A probation service which explicitly serves the community as well as offenders has greater claims to perceived legitimacy; a probation service which could show communities how they gain from the rehabilitation of offenders would have greater claims still.

Rehabilitation and community interests

Instead of rehabilitative programmes being seen primarily as a benefit to offenders, and therefore arguably unfair to those facing similar difficulties who have not offended, we should try to understand rehabilitation as work that offenders undertake as a consequence of a crime: work which is directed to changing their own behaviour and attitudes in a more pro-social direction. A rehabilitative penalty can reflect the interests and values of the wider community and perhaps equip offenders with skills to maintain themselves more effectively and to contribute more to society. The notion of rehabilitation as offenders working to rehabilitate themselves may be better aligned with community values than the notion of offenders simply receiving help, and it may also be more constructive than the attempt to improve public confidence by more rigorous approaches to enforcement.

A concrete way to embody these principles in practice might be to seek to include an explicitly reparative element in every community sentence, or at least in most of those which are substantial enough to warrant the delivery of an accredited programme. Community service has already been conspicuously the most popular reparative penalty (hopefully it will remain so under its new title of community punishment order), and the incorporation of reparative elements in other programmes might confer a greater perceived legitimacy on them. Toch (2000) has argued that the involvement of offenders in altruistic activities can be seen as a form of 'correctional treatment' in itself, offering 'a sense of accomplishment, grounded increments in self-esteem, meaningful purposiveness and obvious restorative implications. Altruistic activity can contribute to cognitive restructuring'. The reparative element need not be large in all cases, and although not resource-neutral it might not be hugely expensive. It might also be unnecessary in those cases where probation orders are still made for 'welfare' reasons. What is important is that it should be noticeable by those to whom it matters.

One possible way of achieving this might be to involve victims, if they wished, in the choice of reparative work to be carried out by the offender. Tendencies to vindictiveness or unrealistic expectations could be controlled by offering a choice between possibilities which had already been assessed as suitable and feasible, and victims would be able to indicate which of the proposed alternatives offered, in their view, the most constructive reparation. Admittedly these proposals involve some blurring of distinctions between other community penalties and community service, but this is already happening through the importation of rehabilitative components and goals into community service; it should still be possible to distinguish between sentences which are primarily reparative and those in which reparation is an element in a wider rehabilitative process. Some similar arguments have been advanced by Todd Clear and his colleagues in relation to reintegrative community justice initiatives in the USA (see, for example, Clear et al. 2000). The central point is to demonstrate that rehabilitation is itself fundamentally restorative and benefits the community as well as the offender.

Learning from social work?

This survey of current developments in community sentences would not be complete without briefly recognizing one development which must generate a certain sense of irony in those who have lived through the repeated efforts of politicians to introduce a gulf between the image of probation and what they take to be the image of social work. In Scotland there has been less perceived need to create this separation (see Smith 1998), but in England and Wales it included the imposition of major changes in probation officers' training in order to end a situation in which they trained alongside social workers. Many probation managers who were initially uneasy about this kind of development have come to embrace it and to endorse the need to abandon 'welfarism'. Certainly there was little prospect of the service achieving its potential contribution to crime reduction and community safety until it came to see itself as a criminal justice resource, but some of the discarded ideas are beginning to reassert themselves in the new context.

Reference has already been made to the concept of 'criminogenic need' which provides a rationale for meeting need, or at least certain needs. It is also increasingly clear that the delivery of effective programmes in the community depends on case management skills to keep offenders involved and to increase the chances of completion. These skills include engagement, motivation, communication and pro-social modelling. Similarly, resettlement work in the community involves mobilizing resources and creating links between offenders and resource systems, and a process of working with offenders on prioritizing and addressing problems which is highly reminiscent of 'task-centred casework' (Reid and Epstein 1972). There have even been indications from Australian research (Trotter 2000) that probation officers with a social work training engage more effectively with the 'What Works' agenda than those with some other backgrounds. Not long ago this would have been heresy, but we hope that the more pragmatic attitude created by the 'What Works' initiative, together with the 'culture of curiosity' (Raynor and Vanstone 2001) which grows from interest in evaluation, evidence and results, will allow a more common-sense approach which draws on useful elements from earlier approaches to probation practice. The next chapter explores what the future may bring.

Further reading

No one book gives a complete overview of community sentences today, but Bottoms *et al.* (2001) is a very useful discussion of current issues by a number of experts. Chapman and Hough (1998) and Harland (1996) provide useful summaries of 'What Works' issues, one from each side of the Atlantic. Trotter (1999) provides a very good account of some issues in effective work and helps to integrate the literature on effective probation with the wider social work literature.

chapter eight

Conclusion: a future for community sentences?

A rational probation service
Penal policy: populism or evidence
Punishment or reintegration?
A sustainable criminal justice policy
Community penalties and the needs of future societies

In the previous chapter we presented an overview of both the status and position of community sentences within the criminal justice and penal systems at the beginning of the twenty-first century. In so doing we attempted to provide a realistic appraisal of not only their achievements but also their inherent problems in the face of a significant increase in accountability and demands for a positive contribution to the resolution of the problem of crime. Those problems, we have argued, have been heightened by their location within a force field of tension between the demands of bureaucratic punitiveness on the one hand, and demonstrable effectiveness on the other, with the result that there is by no means any certainty about whether community sentences can provide answers to questions posed by both criminological and social imperatives. Essentially, those imperatives, we have suggested, invoke a central challenge for policy-makers, politicians, sentencers and practitioners alike, namely to use the lessons of the final quarter of the twentieth century to reformulate the criminal justice system, and thereby the processes of punishment, in a way that leaves it best able to influence offenders towards more pro-social behaviour, and society towards more constructive criminal justice. In turn, that challenge raises critical questions about the future. How far are existent organizational structures and divisions appropriate for the purposes of punishing and helping in the community those who offend? Is there a case for abolition or reformulation of existing agencies? To what extent can those implementing community sentences ensure that policy and practice are actually informed by evidence of what is effective in reducing both crime and the risk posed by crime to the public? Should community sentences continue to supplement prison or should they (and if so can they) be used to replace imprisonment in a significant range of cases as the principal method of protecting the public?

We end this book by attempting to answer or at least stimulate further thinking about those questions, and we do so by reflecting back (within a framework of critical choices) on some of the essential themes of the previous chapters. First, the probation service as a rational organization – developing effectiveness or imposing a centrally developed orthodoxy? Second, the direction of penal policy – driven by populism or evidence? Third, the competing imperatives of punishment and reintegration – enforcement or effective practice? Fourth, the sustainability of criminal justice policy within social cohesion – integration or exclusion? Finally, globalization and crime – separate development or reciprocity?

A rational probation service

Although others have played a part in the implementation of community sentences, the probation service has been at the heart of their development, and the concept of probation has been integral to the notion of keeping offenders out of custodial institutions. As argued in Chapter 2, that notion emerged from a complex relationship between social, political and religious forces extant at a time of significant concern about social degeneration and social order. It took root at the end of the nineteenth and beginning of the twentieth centuries when the offender became an object of interest (Garland 1985; Rose 1985); and it found a place within what Foucault (1977: 74) describes as 'the domain of a whole series of "criminological" sciences and strange "penitentiary" practices'. The justification for community supervision, therefore, was at the same time scientific, political, judicial and moral, but its survival rested on its status as a 'moral good'. How could it be otherwise?

As we described in Chapter 4, for the first fifty years the work that probation officers undertook in the supervision of offenders in the community did not face any critical evaluation, and when it did it appeared invulnerable (Radzinowicz 1958; Wilkins 1958): its survival as a humanizing factor in the criminal justice system seemed assured. Moreover, during this period crime was not the party-political issue it was to become after the 1959 election, and what was important then was the provision of welfare to the disadvantaged who came before the courts. The test of effectiveness, if there was one, was the degree to which it provided the gift of welfare, and reduction of offending was a welcome but not essential by-product; so, the justification for community-based work with offenders lay in the provision of that gift and a belief in its effectiveness.

Chapter 4 outlined how that belief endured enough even in the face of largely negative research findings (Folkard *et al*. 1966, 1976; Lipton *et al*. 1975); how, initially, the service responded (at least at a policy level) by replacing the objective of rehabilitation with that of diversion from custody (Pease *et al*. 1977: Smith, 1982); how rehabilitation was reinstated in policy discourse through the influence of the 'Reasoning and Rehabilitation' research in Canada in the late 1980s and 'social skills and personal problem solving' (Priestley *et al*. 1978, 1984) and the 'offending behaviour' project (McGuire and Priestley 1985) in the United Kingdom; and how that reinstatement received official endorsement through the Pathfinder programmes. The implementation of community supervision, therefore, is focused on the development of effective intervention in the lives of offenders, but does the price of an admittedly positive change have to be the imposition of a centrally developed orthodoxy? Put another way, can the probation service sustain a commitment to rational, reflective and politically and socially accountable policy and practice and at the same time survive as an innovative, flexible and just organization?

We believe that it can, but only if both managers and practitioners are given responsibility, and use that responsibility to ensure that the service within which they work becomes a learning and problem-solving organization. Their ability to do this depends on a genuine interest in 'real-world', continuous evaluation of process as well as content; practitioners committed to a social science approach to their work; partnerships with researchers; and information systems that are owned by practitioners as well as managers and are capable of critical responsiveness. There are encouraging signs that the service is moving in this direction. Some recent surveys of practice referred to earlier (Hedderman and Sugg 1997; Underwood 1998), while revealing problems in both the implementation and evaluation of programmes based on effectiveness principles, identified examples of good practice. Furthermore, more and more services are running programmes accredited for their rigorous subscription to those principles. As Mair (2000) has argued, the dominant influence of the cognitive-behavioural model is potentially problematic. The solving of complex problems associated with offending is dependent on approaches that are responsive to the particular needs and circumstances of each individual situation as well as culturally sensitive: a standardized, routine one-track approach is insufficient. However, what the proliferation of programmes adhering to the basic principles of effective work demonstrates is the capacity of services to be evidence-based in their thinking; so what they need also to sustain is the faculty for critical reflectiveness and self-challenge. They cannot do this alone: the political and social contexts need to reflect those faculties too, and it is to those contexts that we now turn.

Penal policy: populism or evidence

In Chapter 3 we discussed the link between populism as a factor in the way that crime is dealt with at a political level and government-based initiatives such as the Pathfinder project driven by a concern for evidence of effective ways of reducing crime. It is a paradox that illustrates the dilemma facing politicians of both the left and right, namely how they marry their use of crime as a vote-winning device to policies that are demonstrably effective in reducing the risk of people becoming victims of crime. Like it or not, the genie of populism is out of the bottle, and crime and the political response to it will remain an electoral issue; it is the way in which it is shaped that is of fundamental importance. A constructive, measured and evidence-based criminal justice policy requires not only political will but also political courage; moreover, it requires politicians who are prepared to confront the public with the moral and pragmatic arguments against imprisonment and for constructive community sentencing. In alliance with the kind of service outlined above, politicians need to highlight the deficiencies of populist policies. So what direction might a brave new world political agenda take? What might it say?

Ironically, the key to a successful presentation of evidence-driven criminal justice policy might be public protection – the very same fuel of populism. Previously in this book we have attempted to show that the polemic surrounding the use of imprisonment is fraught with difficulties. In the United Kingdom, we suggested, crime has outstripped imprisonment, and rather than increasing, the chances of being imprisoned have decreased. The argument against imprisonment on the grounds of its in-effectiveness is therefore fragile. Instead, we sought more robust arguments in the realm of moral philosophy. Put simply, public protection has to have a moral context. Protecting the public from the harm caused by crime is right because it is consistent with principles of the common good and the right to quality of life. But it also has to be consistent with principles of justice, citizenship and reintegration. The moral integrity of public protection policies is undermined, for instance, if they invoke cruel and unnecessary punishments, if they make offenders worse and less amenable to reintegration, if they harm unintended victims such as prisoners' children or if they have a disproportionate negative effect on ethnic minorities. Public protection through punishment should, therefore, derive its moral justification from its fairness and the successful achievement of its goals.

The new agenda might, therefore, promote a message to the public that when the use of imprisonment is morally justified it should be humane containment premised on properly resourced rehabilitative effort accountable to the rigours of evaluation; and that where a community sentence is considered appropriate it should be applied in a way that provides offenders with the opportunity to rehabilitate themselves and make amends. The test, then, for criminal justice and penal policies should be not whether they are popular but rather whether they are morally justified and effective. The passing of that test by community sentences is linked to the capacity of managers and practitioners in the agencies that administer them to work collaboratively towards the goal of the kind of problem-solving organization referred to above. But it is also dependent on their ability to promote their work effectively both to the relevant parts of the criminal justice system and to the general public. In so doing they might – at last – complete the process of professionalization that began in the early part of the twentieth century. The policy and practice of community supervision of offenders would be informed by a coherent knowledge base derived not simply from experience as in the past but from evidence. Therein lies the best opportunity to establish priorities in the development of community sentences informed by reintegration rather than what some commentators have termed an 'unseemly punitiveness auction' (Drakeford and Vanstone 2000).

Punishment or reintegration?

One of the central arguments of this book has been that the overriding aim of community sentencing should be the reintegration of the offender into the community as a law-abiding citizen, and this argument has been driven by a belief that the reduction or elimination of the harm caused by crime is a moral imperative. Probation and other forms of supervision have no justification without that objective as an ingredient, but this is not to say that concern for the welfare of the individual offender has no place in the canon of probation practice. As the description of the origins and history of community supervision in Chapters 2 and 3, and the elucidation of the politicization of crime in Chapter 5 show, the arguments surrounding sentences such as probation have been framed within a dichotomy of the needs of the offender versus those of the victim. On the one hand the practice of helping offenders has earned the pejorative sobriquet, 'do-gooding', and on the other hand concern for the victim has been subsumed, by some, under right-wing and punitive populism. This is, of course, a crude generalization, but we make it to highlight the fact that often the needs of the offender and victim have been portrayed as separate and irreconcilable, the main exception being the alternative vision presented by the concept of restorative justice.

While acknowledging the positive contribution of restorative justice arguments, here we are concerned to dissolve the dichotomy by endorsing a reduction-of-harm paradigm that simultaneously embraces the needs of offender and victim. This requires a clarification of the relationship between punishment, containment and supervision. The key to that clarification is an acceptance of the idea that people are made subject to community sentences involving supervision as a punishment but not for punishment. Within that explanatory framework punishment is the loss of liberty and restriction flowing from the sentence; containment is the process of monitoring and 'policing' the boundaries of that erosion of liberty; and supervision is the act of trying to reduce the risk of reoffending. As demonstrated in this book, within our paradigm effective reduction of offending, in so far as it must address criminogenic needs, inevitably impacts on the welfare of the offender. Put another way, effective practice entails a focus not only on crime-prone attitudes, beliefs and behaviour but also on crime-related problems such as unemployment, disadvantage emanating from ethnic minority status, shortage of money, drug and alcohol abuse and relationship problems. So, punishment addresses the need of the victim (and the wider community) for justice while supervision addresses the need of the offender to be reintegrated and the need of the victim and future potential victims to be protected. Effective supervision, therefore, ameliorates harm to the offender through problem reduction and harm to future potential victims through crime reduction. Moreover, punishment and reintegration cease to be mutually exclusive, but rather coalesce around the same objective. One part of the deal for criminal justice practitioners such as probation officers is that they retain their adherence to rehabilitation (and inevitably, therefore, their traditional function of providing help) by administering the apparatus of community punishment through enforcement. The other part of the deal is that politicians and policy-makers develop criminal justice policy within a much broader social policy strategy aimed at reducing economic and social conditions conducive to crime and increasing the opportunities for offenders to make crime-free choices and thereby achieve reintegration.

A sustainable criminal justice policy

As some have argued, social policy as an ingredient in the effort to reduce crime has been neglected by successive governments of both the political right and left, thus leaving the offence isolated from 'the personal and relational context which could make it intelligible' (Smith 1997: 2; Drakeford and Vanstone 1996). Moreover, the approach on which the Effective Practice Initiative is based, as we outlined in Chapters 4 and 6, has demonstrated the possibility of one way of reducing crime, but at the same time left itself open to the criticism that its focus on the individual has encouraged a diminution of the importance of work on structural problems such as poverty and unemployment. Moreover, it may have fed the belief that supervision of offenders can in itself be a palliative for crime. But this does not explain why public policy has 'prioritised law and order over social welfare' (Arnold and Jordan 1996). The explanation is more discernible in not only the dominance of the punitive political rhetoric described in Chapter 5 but also the emergence of public policy in which 'the poor, the disturbed, the migrant, disadvantaged ethnic minorities are consistently overpenalised and overimprisoned' (Hudson 1993: 3). We believe this to be a shorthand description of complex political and social processes, but nevertheless it is correct in judging that the penal aspect of this policy drift has contributed to the shaping of what Young (1999) calls 'the exclusive society'.

As we hope that we have demonstrated in this book, the choice facing policy-makers is relatively simple and stark: can they sustain a criminal justice system premised on penal policy that excludes (primarily) the poor? Instead, should it be about social cohesion achieved through criminal and social justice, the reinforcement of prosociality, mutuality and common humanity? If the former, community sentences become minor and ineffective punishments; if the latter, they become one of a range of effective strategies.

The kind of social cohesion we are advocating requires government to resist the inclination to stigmatize and control (through segregation) the troublesome, and to offer a pro-social model expressed through rationality and humanity. However, it also requires those involved in the administering of community sentences to play their own part in promoting social inclusion. In this respect, we are drawn to the strategy advocated by Smith (1997).

He posits social work agencies involved with offenders at the heart of the promotion of social inclusion, and urges them to move 'away from punishment and regulation towards a more generous and optimistic view of what social work with offenders might entail' (p. 6). As we have indicated above, we do not accept that the implementation of community sentences necessarily involves a move away from the regulation of punishment, but we agree with the broad thrust of his argument. The less defensive practice he advocates would feature more accessible offices in the midst of the communities they are meant to serve. Interestingly, one of the findings of the report on the Northumbria Probation Service's reaction to the 1991 Tyneside riots was that the Service had 'withdrawn from the community focus which at one time had characterised its work' (North et al. 1992: 10); and it recommended the setting up of a report centre on the Meadowell Estate. In addition, Smith suggests the use of a more diversified staff group, thus bringing more expertise to bear on the problems associated with crime; the use of a systems or network approach in order to intensify resources; and the development and dissemination of the knowledge drawn from the experience of working with offenders. The model for the collaborative approach he advocates is drawn from the findings of his research on the Freagarrach Project for persistent juvenile offenders in Falkirk and Alloa. While acknowledging the fact that 'community' is a problematical concept, he nevertheless elucidates the sense of optimism emanating from work based on cooperation between social workers, police officers, teachers, volunteers, employers, drug and alcohol workers and staff in colleges. All of this he places within the broader context of Braithwaite's communitarianism and reintegrative shaming, both of which form the basis for an approach that 'connects the values and methods of restorative justice with those of social work' (Smith 1997: 11).

Linked to a concern with effectiveness (what Smith refers to as a component of the 'moral kit' of the worker), these ideas, in our view, represent the best chance of community sentences becoming an important element of the achievement of criminal and social justice. However, as we draw this book to a close, we wish to take them a stage further into the realm of international relationships, and to consider the place of community sentences in societies of the future. In so doing, we suggest that duties to strangers in a globalized society might present an even bigger challenge than crime control.

Community penalties and the needs of future societies

A final question to consider relates to an unresolved debate which has been implicit in many of the controversies and changes of policy and practice which we have documented. In brief, are community penalties or 'punishment in the community' simply another option in the menu of potential punishments, differing from others mainly in the degree of curtailment of liberty, or are they actually or potentially penalties which differ in kind from other penalties? How far do they have distinctive purposes and values, offering a different model for the way society should deal with harmful actions? What might be the benefits or prospects of any alternative model they might represent?

Each of these possibilities has received, in one form or another, some significant support in the past. For example, the creators of the 1991 Criminal Justice Act quite clearly and explicitly positioned 'community sentences' (at that time, for adults, probation orders, community service orders and a combination of the two) as punishments which differed in degree rather than kind. They were for offences 'so serious' that a lesser penalty would not suffice, but not so serious that only a custodial sentence could be passed. There had been a long-standing idea among some probation officers that there was something special about these orders because, unlike other sentences, the offender had to consent in court and so some kind of contract was implied. However, the authors of the 1991 Act saw consent as undermining the perception of these orders as a punishment, or a sentence like other sentences, and therefore standing in the way of their increased use. Eventually, in 1997, the requirement of consent was abolished. On the other hand, other advocates of the increased use of probation and community service had been arguing for some years that such sentences did have the potential to form the basis of a more constructive and problem-solving approach to the consequences of offending.

For example, in response to the first government attempt to define the purposes and objectives of probation services (Home Office 1984), one of the present authors (Raynor 1985) argued that such attempts were in fact consistent with a particular approach to understanding the distinctive purpose of probation and other community sentences. In this approach, the distinctive purpose of community sentencing would be the development of responses to crime which relied less on the coercion of offenders (less, for example, than imprisonment) and more on participation by offenders, and other members of the community, in doing something to repair the consequences of crime. Similar arguments have been advanced by many researchers and practitioners under the banner of 'restorative justice', and have been proposed as an alternative paradigm for responding to crime, including proposals for the constructive involvements of victims to their own benefit and that of the offender. Christie's (1981) arguments that to inflict pain as a consequence of pain simply adds to the total of harm have been followed by Braithwaite's (1989) attempts to use 'reintegrative shaming' to facilitate the offender's recognition of social obligations and the community's acceptance of the rehabilitated offender. ('Rehabilitation' here carries some of its old-fashioned meaning of restoration to the status of full membership of society, as well as its more restricted modern reference to avoiding recidivism.)

It is instructive to consider what these approaches and many other variants of 'restorative' justice (see, for example, Marshall 1999; Miers 2001) have in common. For example, one shared feature is the belief that most offenders, in their capacity as moral agents capable of choice, are joined to the rest of us by common qualities which can in the long run be more important and more influential than the characteristics which divide them from us. Common human needs and capacities provide a basis for communication and influence, and for persuading offenders in various ways to respect the common humanity of others. This can be expressed in various vocabularies and techniques, from training in 'victim awareness' to the improvement of social skills by learning to listen and to appreciate other people's needs and points of view; all of these assume that a dialogue based on common humanity is possible, and this is also assumed by earlier approaches such as moral exhortation or appeals to repentance. Even the attempts by many offenders to justify or excuse offending have been shown to rest on 'neutralization techniques' (Sykes and Matza 1957) which suggest that they share many of society's moral assumptions about crime and need to present their own crime as exceptional or justified by special mitigation ('it doesn't really do any harm', 'they are all insured', 'I had to hit him' and so on). The offenders who get themselves in regular trouble with the law may differ from the rest of us (minor and undetected offenders for the most part) in many respects such as opportunities, resources, social and cognitive skills and acquired beliefs, and they can and do inflict serious harms as a result, but except for a few categories of the most disturbed or abnormal, the promising approaches to these differences are based on communication and on building on similarity.

It has been suggested (e.g. by Pepinsky 1991) that some criminologists see offenders as fundamentally different from themselves; such criminologies are often associated with punitive and stigmatizing approaches to criminal justice. Other criminologists see offenders as basically like ourselves, but with different histories, predicaments and resources. These point to more inclusive approaches. For example, at one time the Home Office systematically discouraged the use of crime prevention advertisements which portrayed offenders as animals (see Smith 1998); this practice was later restored by a more populist and punitive group of ministers. The difference is best understood if we consider what methods of control we see as appropriate against people, compared to those we accept as normal against animal vermin. But do these differences represent anything more than the preferences of human service professionals as opposed to advocates of more robust forms of social control?

Current practice with offenders clearly contains elements of both approaches, and while the available evidence on effectiveness favours those approaches which can enlist the active cooperation of offenders, there is also a clear need for coercive control of the predatory and the dangerous. There are also clear conflicts between these approaches over questions such as the appropriate level of imprisonment or the degree of flexibility needed in the enforcement of community sentences: the progressive loss of flexibility and discretion in this area since the publication of National Standards in 1992 (Home Office 1992) has been insisted on by politicians to counter a perceived 'loss of confidence' in probation services, but is probably reducing the effectiveness of supervision by making it less likely that offenders will complete programmes designed to reduce their offending. In the last analysis, however, choices between these two approaches not only are a matter of evidence but also involve moral and political choices about how we should treat our fellow citizens when they break the law. Our criminal justice processes and systems make a statement about what it means to be a member of our society, and what we believe about the value and potential of human beings (of course, this includes victims as well as offenders). The late Bill McWilliams, in one of his many contributions to probation thinking (McWilliams 1990), argued that probation was not primarily an instrumental activity but an expressive activity: in other words, we should ask not (or not only) what it achieves but what it represents, or what moral commitments and values it embodies and seeks to communicate. Such questions are no longer entirely separate from debates about effectiveness: for example, Bottoms (2001) has recently argued that higher levels of perceived legitimacy in the activities and processes of criminal justice agencies are likely to lead to higher levels of compliance with their requirements (although presumably the main reason for seeking to enhance legitimacy would be that this is right and just, not simply that it might work better). There remains, however, the question of which approach to offenders best expresses or demonstrates a constructive approach to dispute, conflict and harmful acts in society. The debate is no longer between a 'welfare' approach which denies individual responsibility and a 'justice' approach which exaggerates it; rather, it is between those who would communicate with offenders to enlist their own cooperation in changing their offending behaviour, and those who see them simply as the enemy, to be locked away, 'incapacitated' or, worse, used as targets for vindictive anger.

One other response to these questions is to ask ourselves which approach the world is going to need more in the foreseeable future. Are our problems best addressed by division and conflict or by dialogue and communication? This is not a moralistic speculation but a very practical question. Many writers concerned with international affairs and diplomacy (e.g. Burton 1969) have pointed to the pressing need to maintain dialogue and communication even between those whose views and interests appear incompatible, since the search for common ground cannot occur at all in the absence of communication. These are questions of vivid importance as we write this final section in a world dramatically changed by the atrocity in New York on 11 September 2001, and with the first television pictures of the bombing of Afghanistan appearing on our television screens. Of course these dreadful events raise questions far beyond the scope of this book, but they also raise some relevant questions about how societies of the future may need to approach questions of mutual understanding and collective safety. Very soon after 11 September 2001 those policy analysts and commentators who were not simply horrified or vindictive were pointing to the need for a reappraisal of the foreign policies adopted in powerful Western countries; such reappraisals, it was argued, needed to address the glaring inequalities between rich and poor nations and to seek to resolve long-standing conflicts which stood in the way of a collective approach to security (see, for example, Hirst 2001). Western countries were urged, in effect, to be less selfish and to understand better the needs, concerns and interests of the rest of the world. Within a few days we saw a recently elected right-wing American president making decisive interventions to promote negotiations between Israelis and Palestinians (a conflict in which his previous approach had been clearly one-sided) and the beginnings of an international diplomatic effort involving many nations with little history of collaboration or mutual understanding.

Of course these efforts are partly to support a military action which requires the cooperation or at least acquiescence of many nations. However, as the British Prime Minister pointed out to the Labour Party conference soon after the attack on New York (Blair 2001), such international collaboration represents not only a new approach but the only possible approach to a number of problems including international inequalities and regional poverty, as well as the urgent need to address global problems of climate change and depletion of natural resources. In a globalized world no nation state is strong enough to ignore the need for international communication and cooperation, and for effective international institutions. Survival requires that short-term coercive military solutions give way as soon as possible to sustained efforts at international cooperation and problem-solving, and that these should not just be fine words for the present occasion.

Part of our difficulty in addressing such ambitious goals seems to lie in our evolution. Our early experience as a species has left most of us relatively well equipped to perceive and respond to the needs and feelings of those who are close to us or with whom we are in regular contact, particularly if we identify with them as members of the same group. An agenda of global cooperation and mutual support requires us to develop new cultural capacities to respond to the needs of strangers whom we may never meet and with whom we may spontaneously feel little in common. The partial success of welfare states in achieving this within individual nations needs to be generalized to a global level, posing unprecedented challenges to our capacity to identify with the needs and interests of strangers in the face of our customary ignorances and hostilities. The problem is that we seem to have few alternative courses open to us. An even greater challenge lies in the 'green agenda': to prevent ecological disasters we need a better appreciation of the needs and interests of other species, as well as of other members of our own species. Among such huge and global questions, 'punishment in the community' may seem a minor issue, but our prospects of meeting the global challenges seem a little dim if we cannot manage to respond constructively to conflicts and harms within our own communities. Community sentences at their best represent an attempt to cope effectively with crime and disorder by using methods which rely on communication, persuasion, influence, training and positive assistance, with limited coercive powers in reserve and relatively seldom used. These approaches may have much wider applications, and will at least teach us some useful lessons.

References

Adams, S. (1961) Interaction between individual interview therapy and treatment amenability in older youth authority wards, in *Inquiries Concerning Kinds of Treatment for Kinds of Offenders*. Sacramento: California Board of Corrections.

Advisory Council on the Treatment of Offenders (1963) *The Organisation of After-Care*. London: HMSO.

Agozino, B. (1997) *Black Women and the Criminal Justice System*. Aldershot: Ashgate.

Andrews, D.A. and Bonta, J. (1995) *The Level of Service Inventory – Revised Manual*. Toronto: Multi-Health Systems Inc.

Andrews, D.A. and Bonta, J. (1998) *The Psychology of Criminal Conduct*. Cincinnati, OH: Anderson.

Andrews, D.A., Zinger, I., Hoge, R.D. *et al.* (1990) Does correctional treatment work? A clinically relevant and psychologically informed meta-analysis, *Criminology*, 28: 369–404.

Arnold, J. and Jordan, B. (1996) Poverty, in M. Drakeford and M. Vanstone (eds) *Beyond Offending Behaviour*. Aldershot: Arena.

Ashley, P.D. (1962) Group work in the probation setting, *Probation*, 10(1): 6–8.

Aubrey, R. and Hough, M. (1997) *Assessing Offenders' Needs: Assessment Scales for the Probation Service*, Home Office Research Study 166. London: Home Office.

Augustus, J. (1939) *John Augustus, First Probation Officer*. New York: National Probation Association. First published as *A Report of the Labors of John Augustus* by Wright & Hasty, Boston, 1852.

Ayscough, H.H. (1923) *When Mercy Seasons Justice. A Short History of the Works of the Church of England in the Police Courts*. London: Church of England Temperance Society.

Ayscough, H.H. (1929) *The Probation of Offenders*. London: William John Hewitt.

Barr, H. (1966) *A Survey of Group Work in the Probation Service*, Home Office Research Study 9. London: HMSO.

Bartrip, P.W.J. (1975) The career of Matthew Davenport Hill with special reference to his place in penal and educational reform movements in mid-nineteenth century England. PhD thesis, University of Wales, Cardiff.

Bean, P. (1976) *Rehabilitation and Deviance*. London: Routledge & Kegan Paul.

Beck, U. (1992) *Risk Society: Towards a New Modernity*. London: Sage.

Beckett, K. (1997) *Making Crime Pay. Law and Order in Contemporary American Politics*. New York: Oxford University Press.

Beech, A., Fisher, D. and Becket, R. (1998) *STEP 3: An Evaluation of the Prison Sex Offender Treatment Programme*. London: Home Office.

Berntsen, K. and Christiansen, K. (1965) A resocialization experiment with short-term offenders, *Scandinavian Studies in Criminology*, 1: 35–54.

Beveridge, W. (1942) *Social Insurance and Allied Services*, Cmnd. 6404. London: HMSO.

Bilston, W. G. (1961) Group therapy in a probation setting, *Probation*, 9: 150–1.

Blackburn, R. (1980) Still not working? A look at recent outcomes in offender rehabilitation. Paper presented at the Scottish Branch of the British Psychological Society Conference on Deviance, University of Stirling.

Blair, T. (2001) Blair's Speech, *The Guardian*, 3 October: 4–5.

Bochel, D. (1976) *Probation and After-care: Its Development in England & Wales*. Edinburgh: Scottish Academic Press.

Bonta, J. (1993) A summary of research findings on the LSI. Unpublished.

Bonta, J. (1996) Risk-needs assessment and treatment, in A. Harland (ed.) *Choosing Correctional Options that Work*. London: Sage.

Bottoms, A. (1983) Neglected features of contemporary penal systems in D. Garland and P. Young (eds) *The Power to Punish*. London: Heinemann.

Bottoms, A. (1995) The philosophy and politics of punishment and sentencing, in C. Clarkson and R. Morgan (eds) *The Politics of Sentencing Reform*. Oxford: Clarendon Press.

Bottoms, A. (2001) Compliance and community penalties, in A. Bottoms, L. Gelsthorpe and S. Rex (eds) *Community Penalties: Change and Challenges*. Cullompton: Willan.

Bottoms, A.E. and McWilliams, W. (1979) A non-treatment paradigm for probation practice, *British Journal of Social Work*, 9: 159–202.

Bottoms, A.E., Gelsthorpe, L. and Rex, S. (eds) (2001) *Community Penalties: Change and Challenges*, Cullompton: Willan.

Bowpitt, G. (1998) Evangelical Christianity, secular Humanism, and the genesis of British social work, *British Journal of Social Work*, 28: 675–93.

Boyson, R. (ed.) (1971) *Down with the Poor*. London: Churchill.

Braithwaite, J. (1989) *Crime, Shame and Reintegration*. Cambridge: Cambridge University Press.

Broad, B. (1991) *Punishment under Pressure: The Probation Service in the Inner City*. London: Jessica Kingsley.

Broadbent, A. (1989) Poor clients: what can I do?, *Probation Journal*, 36: 151–4.

Brody, S.R. (1976) *The Effectiveness of Sentencing*. London: HMSO.

Brown, A. and Caddick, B. (eds) (1993) *Groupwork with Offenders*. London: Whiting and Birch.

Brown, A. and Seymour, B. (eds) (1984) *Intake Groups for Clients: A Probation Innovation*. Bristol: University of Bristol.

Brownlee, I. (1998) *Community Punishment. A Critical Introduction*. Harlow: Longman.

Bruce, M. (1961) *The Coming of the Welfare State*. London: Batsford.

Burney, E. (1980), *A Chance to Change*. London: National Association for the Care and Resettlement of Offenders.

Burns, Dr (1930) The psychology of the criminal, *Probation*, 1(3): 38–40.

Burton, J. (1969) *Conflict and Communication*. London: Macmillan.

Carr, J. (1913) Probation and its relationship with other agencies, *National Association of Probation Officers*, 3: 28–34.

Cary, Mrs (1913) The value of the probation system as applied to women, *National Association of Probation Officers*, 3: 14–15.

Cary, Mrs (1915) Social clubs for probationers: their needs and objects, *National Association of Probation Officers*, 6: 102–3.

Cavadino, M. and Dignan, J. (1997) *The Penal System: An Introduction*, 2nd edn. London: Sage.

Chapman, T. and Hough, M. (1998) *Evidence-Based Practice*. London: Home Office.

Chinn, H. (1916) Probation work among children, *National Association of Probation Officers*, 7: 123–5.

Chinn, H. (1926) One aspect of the problem of adolescence, *National Association of Probation Officers*, 25: 600–3.

Chinn, H. (1930) A comparative study of probation in America, *Probation*, 1(4): 56–9.

Chinn, H. (1931) Home visiting, *Probation*, 1(6): 84–5.

Christie, N. (1982) *Limits to Pain*. Oxford: Martin Robertson.

Church of England Temperance Chronicle (1873) Canon Ellison's sermon at St. Paul's, 1 May.

Church of England Temperance Society (1901) *The Ninth Annual Report of the London Diocesan Branch of the Church of England Temperance Society*. London: Church of England Temperance Society.

Chute, C.L. (1939) Preface in *John Augustus, First Probation Officer*. London: National Probation Association.

Clark, D. and Howden-Windell, J. (2000) A retrospective study of criminogenic factors in the female prison population. Unpublished report to the Home Office.

Clear, T., Karp, D. and Bruni, J. (2000) Evidence-based practice: a survey of reintegrative community justice initiatives in the USA. Paper presented to the Probation 2000 conference, London.

Cohen, S. (1985) *Visions of Social Control*. Cambridge: Polity Press.

Cooper, E. (1987) Probation practice in the criminal and civil courts, in J. Harding (ed.) *Probation and the Community. A Practice and Policy Reader*. London and New York: Tavistock Publications.

Copas, J.B. (1992) Statistical analysis for a risk of reconviction predictor. Unpublished report to the Home Office.

Coulson, G., Ilacqa, G., Nutbrown, V., Giulekas, D. and Cudjoe, F. (1996) Predictive utility of the LSI for incarcerated female offenders, *Criminal Justice and Behaviour*, 23(3): 427–39.

Crabb, W.C. (1915) Probation officers and probationers: their relation towards each other, *National Association of Probation Officers*, 6: 98–100.

Croft, J. (1978) *Research in Criminal Justice*. London: HMSO.

Croker-King, E. (1915) Juvenile probation, *National Association of Probation Officers*, 5: 66–7.

Daly, K. (1989) Criminal justice ideologies and practices in different voices: some feminist questions about justice, *International Journal of the Sociology of Law*, 17: 1–18.

Dark, S. (1939) *IN AS MUCH ... Christianity in the Police Courts*. London: Student Christian Movement Press.

Davies, M. (1969) *Probationers in their Social Environment*. London: HMSO.

Davies, M. (1974) *Social Work in the Environment*. London: HMSO.

Dawtry, F. (1958) Whither probation?, *British Journal of Delinquency*, 8(3): 180–7.

Denman, G. (1982) *Intensive Intermediate Treatment with Juvenile Offenders: A Handbook of Assessment and Groupwork Practice*, Lancaster: Centre of Youth, Crime and Community, Lancaster University.

Denney, D. (1992) *Racism and Anti-Racism in Probation*. London: Routledge.

Denney, D. and Carrington, B. (1981) Young Rastafarians and the probation service, *Probation Journal*, 28, 4, 111–17.

Ditchfield, J. (1976) *Police Cautioning in England and Wales, HORS 37*. London: HMSO.

Dowden, C. and Andrews, D. (1999) What works for female offenders: a meta-analytic review, *Crime and Delinquency*, 45(4): 438–52.

Downes, D. and Morgan, R. (1997) Dumping the 'hostages to fortune'? The politics of law and order in post-war Britain, in M. Maguire, R. Morgan and R. Reiner (eds) *The Oxford Handbook of Criminology*, 2nd edn. Oxford: Clarendon Press.

Drakeford, M. (1983) Probation: containment or liberty?, *Probation Journal*, 30: 7–10.

Drakeford, M. and Vanstone, M. (eds) (1996) *Beyond Offending Behaviour*. Aldershot: Arena.

Drakeford, M. and Vanstone, M. (2000) Social exclusion and the politics of criminal justice: a tale of two administrations, *Howard Journal*, 39(4): 369–81.

Du Cane, E.F. (1885) *The Punishment and Prevention of Crime*. London: Macmillan.

Ellis, H. (1910) *The Criminal*, 4th edn. London: Blackwood, Scott & Co.

Ellis, T. (2000) Enforcement policy and practice: evidence-based or rhetoric-based? *Criminal Justice Matters*, 39: 6–8.

Farrington, D. (1990) Implications of criminal career research for the prevention of offending, *Journal of Adolescence*, 13: 93–113.

Feeley, M. and Simon, J. (1992) The new penology: notes on the emerging strategy of corrections and its implications, *Criminology*, 30: 449–74.

Fenner, F. (1856) *Raising The Veil; Or, Scenes in the Courts*. Boston: James French & Co.

Fletcher-Cooke, C. (1962) The Morison Report and after, *Probation*, 10(2): 24–9.

Folkard, M.S., Fowles, A.J., McWilliams, B.C. *et al.* (1974) *IMPACT. Intensive Matched Probation and After-Care Treatment. Volume I. The Design of the Probation Experiment and an Interim Evaluation*, Home Office Research Study 24. London: HMSO.

Folkard, M.S., Smith, D.E. and Smith, D.D. (1976) *IMPACT. Intensive Matched Probation and After-Care Treatment. Volume II. The Results of the Experiment*, Home Office Research Study 36. London: HMSO.

Folkard, S., Lyon, K., Carver, M.M. and O'Leary, E. (1966) *Probation Research. A Preliminary Report*. Home Office Research Study 7. London: HMSO.

Foren, R. and Bailey, R. (1968) *Authority in Social Casework*. Oxford: Pergamon Press.

Foucault, M. (1977) *Discipline and Punish. The Birth of the Prison*. London: Penguin Books.

Francis, J.R. (1932) Constructive probation work, *Probation*, 1(11): 168–9.

Friedman, M. (1962) *Capitalism and Freedom*. Chicago: Chicago University Press.

Friends World Committee for Consultation (2000) Offenders and victims: accountability and fairness in the justice process. Statement to United Nations Tenth Congress on the Prevention of Crime and the Treatment of Offenders, Vienna.

Friendship, C., Blud, L., Erikson, M., Travers, R. and Thornton, D. (2001) Cognitive-behavioural treatment for imprisoned offenders: an evaluation of H.M. Prison Services cognitive skills programmes. Report to the Joint Prison/Probation Accreditation Panel.

Frude, N., Honess, T. and Maguire, M. (1990). *CRIME-PICS Handbook*. Cardiff: Michael and Associates.

Frude, N., Honess, T. and Maguire, M. (1994) *CRIME-PICS II Manual*. Cardiff: Michael and Associates.

Fry, M. (1954) The scope for the use for probation, in *European Seminar on Probation*. New York: United Nations.

Fryer, P. (1984) *Staying Power: The History of Black People in Britain*. London: Pluto Press.

Gamon, H.R.P. (1907) *The London Police Court. Today and Tomorrow*. London: J.M. Dent.

Garland, D. (1985) *Punishment and Welfare: A History of Penal Strategies*. Aldershot: Gower.

Garland, D. (1990) *Punishment and Modern Society*. Oxford: Clarendon.

Garland, D. (1997) Probation and the reconfiguration of crime control, in R. Burnett (ed.) *The Probation Service: Responding to Change*, Probation Studies Unit Report 3. Oxford: Centre for Criminological Research.

Garland, D. (2000) The culture of high crime societies: some preconditions of recent law and order policies, *British Journal of Criminology*, 40: 347–75.

Gelsthorpe, L. (2001) Accountability: difference and diversity in the delivery of community penalties, in A. Bottoms, L. Gelsthorpe and S. Rex (eds) *Community Penalties: Change and Challenges*. Cullompton: Willan.

Gendreau, P. and Ross, R. (1980) Effective correctional treatment: bibliotherapy for cynics, in R. Ross and P. Gendreau (eds) *Effective Correctional Treatment*. Toronto: Butterworths.

Giddens, A. (1998) *The Third Way: the Renewal of Social Democracy*. Cambridge: Polity.

Glueck, S. (ed.) (1933) *Probation and Criminal Justice. Essays in Honor of Herbert C. Parsons*. New York: Macmillan.

Glueck, S. (1939) *Introduction*, in *John Augustus, First Probation Officer*. National Probation Association.

Goldblatt, P. and Lewis, C. (1998) *Reducing Offending: an Assessment of Research Evidence on Ways of Dealing with Offending Behaviour*, Home Office Research Study 187. London: Home Office.

Goldstone, H. (1932) Economic causes of crime, *Probation*, 1(12): 185–6.

Goring, C. (1919) *The English Convict*, abridged edn. London: HMSO.

Grinnell, F.W. (1941) The common law history of probation. An illustration of the 'equitable' growth of criminal law, *Journal of Criminal Law and Criminology*, 32(1): 70–91.

Gwym, S.A. (1941) Causes of delinquency, *Probation*, 3(16): 226–7.

Haines, K. (1998) Some principled objections to a restorative justice approach to working with juvenile offenders, in L. Walgrave (ed.) *Restorative Justice for Juveniles*. Leuven: Leuven University Press.

Halliday, J. (2001) *Making Punishments Work*. London: Home Office.

Hansard (1886) *Probation of First Offenders Bill. Second Reading. House of Commons*. Vol. 305, Cols 333–9. London: Cornelius Buck & Son.

Harland, A. (ed.) (1996) *Choosing Correctional Options that Work*. London: Sage.

Harris, R.J. (1992) *Crime, Criminal Justice and the Probation Service*. London: Routledge.

Harrison, B. (1971) *Drink and the Victorians. The Temperance Question in England 1815–72*. London: Faber and Faber.

Hatcher, R. and McGuire, J. (2001) *Report on the Psychometric Evaluation of the Think-First Programme in Community Settings*. Liverpool: University of Liverpool Department of Clinical Psychology.

Hayek, F. (1944) *The Road to Serfdom*. London: Routledge.

Hedderman, C. and Sugg, D. (1997) *The Influence of Cognitive Approaches, with a Survey of Probation Programmes, Part 2*. Home Office Research Study 171. London: Home Office.

Heidensohn, F. (1986) Models of justice: Portia or Persephone? Some thoughts on equality, justice, gender and fairness in the field of criminal justice, *International Journal of the Sociology of Law*, 14: 187–98.

Helmsley, Mr (1915) Juvenile crime: some causes and remedies, *National Association of Probation Officers*, 6: 100–2.

Hemsley, Mrs (1920) Probation from a women's outlook, *National Association of Probation Officers*, 12: 221–2.

Her Majesty's Inspectorate of Probation (1995) *Dealing with Dangerous People: the Probation Service and Public Protection*. London: Home Office.

Her Majesty's Inspectorate of Probation (2000) *Towards Race Equality*. London: Home Office.

Hill, M. D. (1857) *Suggestions for the Repression of Crime Contained in Charges Delivered to the Grand Juries of Birmingham Supported by Additional Facts and Arguments: Together with Articles from Reviews and Newspapers Controverting or Advocating the Conclusions of the Author*. London: John. W. Parker and Son.

Hirst, D. (2001) The shame of Palestine, *The Guardian*, 23 September: 16.

Hodson, C.B.S. (1932) Biological aspects of crime, *Probation*, 1(10): 151–2.

Hollin, C. (1995) The meaning and implications of programme integrity, in J. McGuire (ed.) *What Works: Reducing Offending*. Chichester: Wiley.

Holmes, R. (1915) *My Police Court Friends with the Colours*. Edinburgh and London: William Blackwood and Sons.

Holmes, R. (1923) *Them that Fall*. Edinburgh and London: William Blackwood and Sons.

Holmes, T. (1902) *Pictures and Problems from London Police Courts*. London: Edward Arnold.

Holmes, T. (1908) *Known to the Police*. London: Edward Arnold.

Holmes, T. (1912) *Psychology and Crime*. London: J. M. Dent and Sons.

Home Office (1909) *Report of the Departmental Committee on the Probation of Offenders Act*. London: HMSO.

Home Office (1927) *Report of the Departmental Committee on the Treatment of Young Offenders* Cmd. 2831. London: HMSO.

Home Office (1962) *Report of the Departmental Committee on the Work of the Probation Service*, Cmnd. 1650. London: HMSO

Home Office (1968) *Children in Trouble*, Cmnd 3601. London: HMSO.

Home Office (1970) *Report of the Advisory Council on the Penal System. Non-Custodial and Semi-Custodial Penalties*. London: HMSO.

Home Office (1984) *Probation Service in England and Wales: Statement of National Objectives and Priorities*. London: Home Office.

Home Office (1988a) *Punishment, Custody and the Community*, Cm. 424. London: HMSO.

Home Office (1988b) *The Parole System in England and Wales: Report of the Review Committee*, Cm. 532. London: HMSO.

Home Office (1990a) *Crime, Justice and Protecting the Public*, Cm. 965. London: HMSO.

Home Office (1990b) *Supervision and Punishment in the Community*, Cm. 966. London: HMSO.

Home Office (1992) *National Standards for the Supervision of Offenders in the Community*. London: Home Office.

Home Office (1993) *The National Risk of Reconviction Predictor*. London: Home Office Research and Planning Unit.

Home Office (1995a) *National Standards for the Supervision of Offenders in the Community*. London: Home Office.

Home Office (1995b). *Managing What Works: Conference Report and Guidance on Critical Success Factors for Probation Supervision Programmes*, Circular 77/1995. London: Home Office.

Home Office (1996) *Guidance for the Probation Service on the Offender Group Reconviction Scale*, Circular 63/1996. London: Home Office.

Home Office (1998) *Effective Practice Initiative. National Implementation Plan for the Supervision of Offenders*. Circular 35/1998. London: HMSO.

Home Office (1999). *What Works: Reducing Re-offending: Evidence-based Practice*. London: Home Office.

Home Office (2000a) *A Review of the Sentencing Framework*. London: Home Office.

Home Office (2000b) *The National Standards for the Supervision of Offenders in the Community*, 3rd revision. London: Home Office.

Home Office (2001) *Probation Statistics England and Wales 1999*. London: Home Office.

Hood, R. (1974) *Tolerance and the Tariff*. London: National Association for the Care and Resettlement of Offenders.

Hood, R (1992) *Race and Sentencing: A Study in the Crown Court*. Oxford: Clarendon Press.

Howard Association (1867) *Annual Report*. London: Howard Association.

Howard Association (1868) *Annual Report*. London: Howard Association.

Howard Association (1878) *Annual Report*. London: Howard Association.

Howard Association (1881) *Annual Report.* London: Howard Association.
Howard Association (1882) *Annual Report.* London: Howard Association.
Howard Association (1883) *Annual Report.* London: Howard Association.
Howard Association (1884) *Annual Report.* London: Howard Association.
Howard Association (1902) *Annual Report.* London: Howard Association.
Howard Association (1903) *Annual Report.* London: Howard Association.
Howard Association (1905) *Annual Report.* London: Howard Association.
Howard Association (1906) *Annual Report.* London: Howard Association.
Hudson, B.A. (1987) *Justice through Punishment: A Critique of the 'Justice Model' of Corrections.* London: Macmillan
Hudson, B.A. (1993) *Penal Policy and Social Justice.* London: Macmillan.
Hudson, B.A. (1996) *Understanding Justice: An Introduction to the Ideas, Perspectives and Controversies in Modern Penal Theory.* Buckingham: Open University Press.
Hudson, B.L. (1988) Social skills training in practice, *Probation Journal,* 35(3): 85–91.
Hughes, E.P. (1903) *The Probation System of America.* London: The Howard Association.
Hugman, B. (1980) Radical practice in probation, in M. Brake and R. Bailey (eds) *Radical Social Work and Practice.* London: Edward Arnold.
Humphrey, C. and Pease, K. (1992) Effectiveness measurement in the probation service: a view from the troops, *Howard Journal of Criminal Justice,* 31: 31–52.
Hunt, A.W. (1964) Enforcement in probation casework, *British Journal of Delinquency* 4: 239–52.
Ignatieff, M. (1978) *A Just Measure of Pain. The Penitentiary in the Industrial Revolution 1750–1850.* New York: Pantheon.
Izzo, R. and Ross, R. (1990) Meta-analysis of rehabilitation programs for juvenile delinquents, *Criminal Justice and Behaviour,* 17: 134–42.
Jarvis, F. (1972) *Advise, Assist and Befriend: A History of the Probation and After-Care Service.* London: National Association of Probation Officers.
Jenkins, J. and Lawrence, D. (1992) Black Groups Initiative review. Unpublished paper, Inner London Probation Service.
Johnson, A. (ed.) (1928) *Dictionary of American Biography.* London: Oxford University Press.
Joint Prison/Probation Accreditation Panel (2000) *What Works: First Report from the Joint Prison/Probation Accreditation Panel 1999–2000.* London: Home Office. www.homeoffice.gov.uk/cpd/probu/jppapar.pdf (accessed 29 November 2001).
Jones, A., Kroll, B., Pitts, J., Smith, P. and Weise, J. L. (1992) *The Probation Handbook.* London: Longman.
Jones, H. (1962) The group approach to treatment, *Howard Journal,* 11(1): 58–63.
Jones, M., Mordecai, M., Rutter, F. and Thomas, L. (1993) A Miskin model of groupwork with women offenders, in A. Brown and B. Caddick (eds) *Groupwork with Offenders.* London: Whiting and Birch.
Jordan, B. (2000) *Social Work and the Third Way: Tough Love as Social Policy.* London: Sage.
Jordan, W. and Jones, M. (1988) Poverty, the underclass and probation practice, *Probation Journal,* 36: 123–7.

Kemshall, H. (1996) Reviewing risk: a review of research on the assessment of risk and dangerousness: implications for policy and practice in the Probation Service. Unpublished report to the Home Office Research and Statistics Directorate.

Kemshall, H. and Maguire, M. (2001) Public protection, partnership and risk penality: the multi-agency risk management of sexual and violent offenders, *Punishment and Society* 3: 237–64.

Kennedy, J.E.R. (1941) Mother and child, *Probation*, 3(16): 225–6.

Kent Probation and After-Care Service (1981) Probation Control Unit: a community-based experiment in intensive supervision, in *Annual Report on the Work of the Medway Centre*. Maidstone: Kent Probation and After-Care Service.

King, J. (1969) *The Probation and After-Care Service*, 3rd edn. London: Butterworth.

Le Mesurier, L. (1935) *A Handbook of Probation*. London: National Association of Probation Officers.

Leeson, C. (1914) *The Probation System*. London: P.S. King and Son.

Lipsey, M. (1992) Juvenile delinquency treatment: a meta-analytic enquiry into the variability of effects, in T. Cook, H. Cooper, D.S. Cordray, *et al.* (eds) *Meta-Analysis for Explanation: A Case-Book*. New York: Russell Sage.

Lipsey, M. (1995) What do we learn from 400 research studies on the effectiveness of treatment with juvenile delinquents?, in J. McGuire (ed.) *What Works: Reducing Offending*. Chichester: Wiley.

Lipton, D., Martinson, R. and Wilks, J. (1975). *The Effectiveness of Correctional Treatment*. New York: Praeger.

Lloyd, C., Mair, G. and Hough, M. (1994) *Explaining Reconviction Rates: A Critical Analysis*. London: HMSO.

MacDonald, G. (1993) Developing empirically-based practice in probation, *British Journal of Social Work*, 24, 405–27.

Maguire, M. and Raynor, P. (1997) The revival of throughcare: rhetoric and reality in automatic conditional release, *British Journal of Criminology*, 37, 1: 1–14.

Maguire, M., Raynor, P., Vanstone, M. and Kynch, J. (2000) Voluntary after-care and the probation service: a case of diminishing responsibility, *Howard Journal of Criminal Justice* 39: 234–48.

Mair, G. (1986) Ethnic minorities, police and the magistrates court, *British Journal of Criminology*, 46: 147–55.

Mair, G. (1988) *Probation Day Centres*. London: HMSO.

Mair, G. (1995) Standing at the crossroads: what works in community penalties, in Home Office *Managing What Works: Conference Report and Guidance on Critical Success Factors for Probation Supervision Programmes*, Circular 77/1995. London: Home Office.

Mair, G. (1997) Community penalties and probation, in M. Maguire, R. Morgan and R. Reiner (eds) *The Oxford Handbook of Criminology*, 2nd edn. Oxford: Clarendon Press.

Mair, G. (2000) Credible accreditation?, *Probation Journal*, 47: 268–71.

Marshall, T. (1999) *Restorative Justice: An Overview*. London: Home Office.

Martinson, J. (1974) What works? Questions and answers about prison reform, *The Public Interest*, 35: 22–54.

Martinson, R. (1979) New findings, new views: a note of caution regarding sentencing reform, *Hofstra Law Review* 7: 243–58.

Masters, G. and Smith, D. (1998) Portia and Persephone revisited: thinking about feeling in criminal justice, *Theoretical Criminology*, 2(1): 5–27.

Mathiesen, T. (1983) The future of control systems. The case of Norway, in D. Garland and P. Young (eds) *The Power to Punish: Contemporary Penality and Social Analysis*. London: Heinemann.

Matza, D. (1964) *Delinquency and Drift*. New York: Wiley.

May, C. (1999) *Explaining Reconviction Following a Community Sentence: The Role of Social Factors*, Home Office Research Study 192. London: Home Office.

May, T. (1991a) *Probation: Politics, Policy and Practice*. Buckingham: Open University Press.

May, T. (1991b) Under siege: probation in a changing environment, in R. Reiner and M. Cross (eds) *Beyond Law and Order*. London: Macmillan.

May, T. (1994) Probation and community sanctions, in M. Maguire, R. Morgan and R. Reiner (eds) *The Oxford Handbook of Criminology*. Oxford: Clarendon Press.

May, T. and Vass, A.A. (eds) (1996) *Working with Offenders: Issues, Contexts and Outcomes*. London: Sage.

Mayling, G.H. (1933) Probation officers' investigations, *Probation*, 1(14): 217–19.

McCullough, M.K. (1962) The practice of groupwork in a hostel, *Probation*, 10(3): 36–7.

McGuire, J. (ed.) (1995) *What Works: Reducing Offending*. Chichester: Wiley.

McGuire, J. (2000) *Cognitive-Behavioural Approaches*. London: Home Office.

McGuire, J. and Priestley, P. (1985) *Offending Behaviour: Skills and Stratagems for Going Straight*. London: Batsford.

McGuire, J., Broomfield, D., Robinson, C. and Rowson, B. (1995) Short-term impact of probation programs: an evaluative study, *International Journal of Offender Therapy and Comparative Criminology*, 39: 23–42.

McIvor, G. (1990) *Sanctions for Serious or Persistent Offenders*. Stirling: Social Work Research Centre.

McIvor, G. (1991) Social work intervention in community service, *British Journal of Social Work*, 21: 591–609.

McIvor, G. (1992) *Sentenced to Serve*. Aldershot: Avebury.

McLaren, K. (1992) *Reducing Reoffending: What Works Now?* Wellington, NZ: Department of Justice.

McWilliams, W. (1983) The Mission to the English police courts 1876–1936, *Howard Journal of Criminal Justice*, 22: 129–47.

McWilliams, W. (1985) The Mission transformed: professionalism of probation between the wars, *Howard Journal of Criminal Justice*, 24: 257–74.

McWilliams, W. (1986) The English probation system and the diagnostic ideal, *Howard Journal of Criminal Justice*, 25: 241–60.

McWilliams, W. (1987) Probation, pragmatism and policy, *Howard Journal of Criminal Justice*, 26: 97–121.

McWilliams, W. (1990) Probation practice and the management ideal, *Probation Journal*, 37: 60–7.

McWilliams, W. and Pease, K. (1990) Probation practice and an end to punishment, *Howard Journal of Criminal Justice*, 29: 14–24.

Membury, S.J. (1922) Brothers, we are builders of men, *National Association of Probation Officers*, 17: 345–6.

Merrington, S. and Stanley, S. (2000) Doubts about the What Works Initiative, *Probation Journal*, 47: 272–5.

Miers, D. (2001) *An International Review of Restorative Justice*, Crime Reduction Research Series Paper 10. London: Home Office.

Miers, D., Maguire, M., Goldie, S. *et al.* (2001) *An Exploratory Evaluation of Restorative Justice Schemes*, Crime Reduction Series Paper 9. London: Home Office.

Minn, W.G. (1950) Probation work, in C. Morris (ed.) *Social Casework in Great Britain*. London: Faber and Faber.

Monger, M. (1964) *Casework in Probation*. London: Butterworth.

Moreland, D.W. (1941) John Augustus and his successors, *National Association Yearbook*, 1–23.

Morris, A. and Giller, H. (eds) (1983) *Providing Criminal Justice for Children*. London: Edward Arnold.

Muirhead, J.H. (1914) Introduction, in C. Leeson, *The Probation System*. London: P.S. King and Son.

National Association of Discharged Prisoners' Aid Societies (1956) *Handbook*. London: NADPAS.

National Probation Service (2001) *A New Choreography*. London: Home Office.

Nellis, M. (1995) Probation values for the 1990s, *Howard Journal of Criminal Justice*, 34: 19–44.

Newburn, T. (1995) *Crime and Criminal Justice Policy*. Harlow: Longman.

Newton, G. (1956) Trends in probation training, *British Journal of Delinquency*, 7(2): 123–35.

North, J., Adair, H., Langley, B., Mills, J. and Morten, G. (1992) *The Dog that Finally Barked: The Tyneside Disturbances of 1991, a Probation Perspective*. Internal document, Northumbria Probation Service.

Northumbria Probation Service (1994) *Survey of Probation Practice on Poverty Issues*. Internal document, Northumbria Probation Service.

OASys Project Team (1999) *The Offender Assessment System (OASys) Manual*. London: Home Office.

Osler, A. (1995) *Introduction to the Probation Service*. Winchester: Waterside Press.

Page, M. (1992) *Crime Fighters of London. A History of the Origins and Development of the London Probation Service 1876–1965*. London: Inner London Probation Service Development Trust.

Palin, J. (1915) Homes, rescue and prevention, in connection with probation work, *National Association of Probation Officers*, 6: 88–9.

Palmer, T. (1974) The Youth Authority's Community Treatment Project, *Federal Probation*, 38: 3–14.

Palmer, T. (1975) Martinson revisited, *Journal of Research in Crime and Delinquency*, 12: 133–52.

Parker, K. and Bilston, W. G. (1959) Belmont: a therapeutic opportunity, *Probation*, 9(3): 36–7.

Paskell, W. (1954) Probation casework: basic principles and methods, in *European Seminar on Probation*. New York: United Nations.

Pearson, G. (1983) *Hooligan. A History of Respectable Fears*. London: Macmillan.

Pease, K. and McWilliams, W. (eds) (1980) *Community Service by Order*. Edinburgh: Scottish Academic Press.

Pease, K., Billingham, S. and Earnshaw, I. (1977) *Community Service Assessed in 1976*, Home Office Research Study 39. London: HMSO.

Pepinsky, H. (1991) Peacemaking in criminology and criminal justice, in H. Pepinsky and R. Quinney (eds) *Criminology as Peacemaking*. Bloomington: Indiana University Press.

Pepinsky, H. and Quinney, R. (eds) (1991) *Criminology as Peacemaking*. Bloomington: Indiana University Press.

Percival, F.W. (1941) The problem of juvenile delinquency, *Probation*, 3(16): 227–8.

Petersilia, J. (1990) Conditions that permit intensive supervision programmes to survive, *Crime and Delinquency*, 36: 126–45.

Pickersgill-Cunliffe, Miss (1913) *Opinions and hints on rescue work. Notes on Work Amongst the Fallen and the Cautionary List*. London April 1913 Annual Conference.

Pitts, J. (1992) The end of an era, *Howard Journal of Criminal Justice,* 31: 133–49.

Pointing, J. (ed.) (1986) *Alternatives to Custody*. Oxford: Blackwell.

Potter, J. Hasloch (1927*) IN AS MUCH. The Story of the Police Court Mission 1876–1926*. London: Williams and Northgate.

Potts, W.A. (1903) The problem of the morally defect. A paper read at the recent Conference on the Care of the Feeble-minded at the Guildhall. *Notes on Work Amongst the Fallen and the Cautionary List*.

Potts, W.A. (1928) The medical aspects of delinquency, *National Association of Probation Officers*, 8: 671–3.

Poulton, F. (1925) The spiritual factor in probation work, *National Association of Probation Officers*, 23: 546–7.

Priestley, P., McGuire, J., Flegg, D., Hemsley, V. and Welham, D. (1978) *Social Skills and Personal Problem Solving. A Handbook of Methods*. London: Tavistock.

Priestley, P., McGuire, J., Flegg, D., Hemsley, D., Welham, D., and Barnitt, R. (1984) *Social Skills in Prisons and in the Community*. London: Routledge & Kegan Paul.

Radzinowicz, L. (ed.) (1958) *The Results of Probation. A Report of the Cambridge Department of Criminal Science*. London: MacMillan & Co.

Raeburn, W. (1958) Probation was made for man, *British Journal of Delinquency*, 7(3): 162–79.

Rankin, C. (1921) The problem of the difficult case, *National Association of Probation Officers*, 16: 321–3.

Rawlings, P. (1999) *Crime and Power. A History of Criminal Justice 1688–1998*. London: Longman.

Raynor, P. (1985) *Social Work, Justice and Control*. Oxford: Blackwell.

Raynor, P. (1988) *Probation as an Alternative to Custody*. Aldershot: Avebury.

Raynor, P. (1997) Some observations on rehabilitation and justice, *Howard Journal*, 36(3): 248–62.

Raynor, P. (1998) Attitudes, social problems and reconvictions in the STOP probation experiment, *Howard Journal*, 37: 1–15.

Raynor, P. and Vanstone, M. (1994a) Probation, practice effectiveness and the non-treatment paradigm, *British Journal of Social Work*, 24: 387–404.

Raynor, P., and Vanstone, M. (1994b) *Straight Thinking On Probation: Third Interim Evaluation Report: Reconvictions within 12 Months*, Bridgend: Mid Glamorgan Probation Service.

Raynor, P. and Vanstone, M. (1996) Reasoning and Rehabilitation in Britain: the results of the Straight Thinking On Probation (STOP) programme, *International Journal of Offender Therapy and Comparative Criminology*, 40: 272–84.

Raynor, P. and Vanstone, M. (1997) *Straight Thinking On Probation (STOP): The Mid Glamorgan Experiment*, Probation Studies Unit Report No. 4. University of Oxford Centre for Criminological Research.

Raynor, P. and Vanstone, M. (2001) Straight Thinking On Probation: evidence-based practice and the culture of curiosity, in G. Bernfeld, D. Farrington and A. Leschied (eds) *Offender Rehabilitation in Practice*. Chichester: Wiley.

Raynor, P., Smith, D. and Vanstone, M. (1994) *Effective Probation Practice*. Basingstoke: Macmillan.

Raynor, P., Roberts, C., Kynch, J. and Merrington, M. (2000) *Risk and Need Assessment in Probation Services: An Evaluation*, Home Office Research Study 211. London: Home Office.

Reid, W.J. and Epstein, L. (1972) *Task Centred Casework*. New York: Columbia University Press.

Reinventing Probation Council (2000) *Transforming Probation through Leadership: the Broken Windows Model*. New York: Manhattan Institute. www.manhattan-institute.org/broken_windows.pdf (accessed 28 November 2001).

Restorative Justice Consortium (2000) *Restorative Justice from Margins to Mainstream*. London: Restorative Justice Consortium.

Rex, S. and Matravers, A. (eds) (1998) *Pro-Social Modelling and Legitimacy*. Cambridge: Institute of Criminology.

Roberts, C. (1989) *Hereford and Worcester Probation Service Young Offender Project: First Evaluation Report*. Oxford: Department of Social and Administrative Studies.

Roberts, C., Burnett, R., Kirby, A. and Hamill, H. (1996) *A System for Evaluating Probation Practice*, Probation Studies Unit Report 1. Oxford: Centre for Criminological Research.

Robinson, G. (2001) Power, knowledge and What Works in probation, *Howard Journal* 40: 235–54.

Rock, P. (1990) *Helping Victims of Crime*. Oxford: Oxford University Press.

Rose, G. (1961) *The Struggle for Penal Reform. The Howard League and its Predecessors*. London: Stevens and Sons.

Rose, N. (1985) *The Psychological Complex. Psychology, Politics and Society in England, 1869–1939*. London: Routledge & Kegan Paul.

Rose, N. (1996) Psychiatry as a political science: advanced liberalism and the administration of risk, *History of the Human Sciences*, 9(2): 1–23.

Ross, R.R. and Fabiano, E.A. (1985) *Time to Think: A Cognitive Model of Delinquency Prevention and Offender Rehabilitation*. Johnson City, TN: Institute of Social Sciences and Arts.

Ross, R.R., Fabiano, E.A. and Ross, R.D. (1986) *Reasoning and Rehabilitation: A Handbook for Teaching Cognitive Skills*. Ottawa: University of Ottawa.

Ross, R.R., Fabiano, E.A. and Ewles, C.D. (1988) Reasoning and rehabilitation,

International Journal of Offender Therapy and Comparative Criminology, 32: 29–35.

Rowson, B. and McGuire, J. (eds) (1992) *What Works: Effective Methods to Reduce Offending*.

Rumgay, J. (1989) Talking tough: empty threats in probation practice, *Howard Journal of Criminal Justice*, 28: 177–86.

Rutherford, A. (1986) *Growing Out of Crime*. Harmondsworth: Penguin.

Rutherford, A. (1997) Criminal policy and the eliminative ideal, *Social Policy and Administration*, 31: 116–35.

Rutherford, A. (1993) *Criminal Justice and the Pursuit of Decency*. Oxford: Oxford University Press.

Saleilles, R. (1911) *The Individualization of Punishment*, translated from the 2nd French edition by Rachel Szold Jastrow. London: William Heinemann.

Sarno, C., Hough, M., Nee, C. and Herrington, V. (1999) *Probation Employment Schemes in Inner London and Surrey – An Evaluation*, Research Findings 89, Home Office Research, Development and Statistics Directorate. London: Home Office.

Saskatchewan Newstart (1969) *Life Skills Coaching Manual*. Prince Albert, Sask.: Training Research and Development Station, Department of Manpower and Immigration.

Scraton, P. (ed.) (1987) *Law, Order and the Authoritarian State*. Milton Keynes: Open University Press.

Seddon, M. (1979) Clients as social workers, in D. Brandon and B. Jordan (eds) *Creative Social Work*. Oxford: Blackwell.

Seebohm, F. (Chair) (1968) *Report of the Committee on Local Authority and Allied Personal Social Services*, Cmnd. 3703. London: HMSO.

Shaw, M. (1974) *Social Work in Prison*. London: HMSO.

Shaw, M. and Hannah-Moffatt, K. (2000) Gender, diversity and risk assessment in Canadian corrections, *Probation Journal*, 47(3): 163–72.

Sinclair, I. (1971) *Hostels for Probationers*, Home Office Research Study 6. London: HMSO.

Singer, L.R. (1991) A non-punitive paradigm for probation practice: some sobering thoughts, *British Journal of Social Work*, 21: 611–26.

Smith, D. (1995) *Criminology for Social Work*. Basingstoke: Macmillan.

Smith, D. (1998) Social work with offenders: the practice of exclusion and the potential for inclusion, in M. Barry and C. Hallett (eds) *Social Exclusion and Social Work*. Lyme Regis: Russell House.

Smith, D. J. (1997) Ethnic origins, crime and criminal justice, in M. Maguire, R. Morgan and R. Reiner (eds) *The Oxford Handbook of Criminology*. Oxford: Clarendon Press.

Smith, D. (2000) Learning from the Scottish juvenile justice system, *Probation*, 47(1): 12–17.

Smith, L.J.F. (1982) *Day Training Centres*, Home Office Research Bulletin No 14: 34–7.

Stewart, G., Stewart, J., Prior, A. and Peelo, M. (1989) *Surviving Poverty: Probation Work and Benefits Policy*. Wakefield: Association of Chief Probation Officers.

Stewart, J., Smith, D.B., Stewart, G. and Fullwood, C. (1994) *Understanding Offending Behaviour*. London: Longman.

Sullivan, M. (1994) *Modern Social Policy*. London: Harvester Wheatsheaf.

Suttie, Dr I.D. (1930) Normal offenders, *Probation*, 1(5): 69–70.

Sykes, G. and Matza, D. (1957) Techniques of neutralization: a theory of delinquency, *American Sociological Review*, 22: 664–70.

Talbot, N.S. (1934) Influence and the probation officer, *Probation*, 1(18): 273–4.

Tallack, W. (1871) *Humanity and Humanitarianism. The Question of Criminal Lunacy and Capital Punishment*. London: F.B. Kitto.

Tallack, W. (1872) *Defects in the Criminal Administration and Penal Legislation of Great Britain and Ireland. With Remedial Suggestions*. London: F.B. Kitto.

Tallack, W. (1984) *Penological and Preventative Principles*. New York and London: Garland Publishing, Inc. First published by Wertheimer, Lea and Co., London, 1889.

Taylor, D. (1998) *Crime, Policing and Punishment in England, 1750–1914*. New York: St Martin's Press.

Thornton, D. (1987) Treatment effects on recidivism: a reappraisal of the nothing works doctrine, in B. McGurk, D. Thornton and M. Williams (eds) *Applying Psychology to Imprisonment: Theory and Practice*. London: HMSO.

Thorpe, D. (1978) Intermediate treatment, in N. Tutt (ed.) *Alternative Strategies for Coping with Crime*. Oxford: Blackwell and Robertson.

Thorpe, D.H., Smith, D., Green, C.J. and Paley, J. (1980) *Out of Care*. London: Allen & Unwin.

Thorpe, J. (1979) *Social Inquiry Reports: A Survey*. London: HMSO.

Timasheff, N.S. (1941) *One Hundred Years of Probation 1841–1941. Part One: Probation in the United States, England and the Commonwealth of Nations*. New York: Fordham University Press.

Toch, H. (2000) Altruistic activity as correctional treatment, *International Journal of Offender Therapy and Comparative Criminology*, 44: 270–8.

Todd, M. (1964) *Ever Such a Nice Lady. The Experiences – Rich in 'Human Appeal' – of a Juvenile Court and Bow Street Probation Officer*. London: Victor Gollancz.

Trotter, C. (1993) *The Supervision of Offenders – What Works? A Study Undertaken in Community Based Corrections*. Melbourne: Victoria Department of Justice.

Trotter, C. (1999) *Working with Involuntary Clients*. London: Sage.

Trotter, C. (2000) Social work education, pro-social modelling and effective probation practice, *Probation Journal*, 47: 256–61.

Trought, Mr (1925) Probation work as a profession, *National Association of Probation Officers*, 22: 509–10.

Turnbull, P., McSweeney, T., Webster, R., Edmunds, M. and Hough, M. (2000) *Drug Treatment and Testing Orders: Final Evaluation Report*, Home Office Research Study 212. London: Home Office.

Underdown, A. (1995) *Effectiveness of Community Supervision: Performance and Potential*. Manchester: Greater Manchester Probation Service.

Underdown, A. (1998) *Strategies for Effective Supervision: Report of the HMIP What Works Project*. London: Home Office.

Vanstone, M. (1985) Moving away from help? Policy and practice in probation day centres, *Howard Journal of Criminal Justice*, 24(1): 20–8.

Vanstone, M. (1993) A missed opportunity reassessed: the influence of the Day Training Centre experiment on the criminal justice system and probation practice, *British Journal of Social Work*, 23: 213–29.

Vanstone, M. (2000) Cognitive-behavioural work with offenders in the UK: a history of influential endeavour, *Howard Journal of Criminal Justice*, 39(2): 171–83.

Vanstone, M. (2001) Making sense of probation: a history of professional discourse. PhD thesis, University of Wales.

Vanstone, M. and Raynor, P. (1981), Diversion from prison – a partial success and a missed opportunity, *Probation Journal*, 28: 85–9.

Vass, A.A. (1990) *Alternatives to Prison: Punishment, Custody and the Community*. London, Sage.

Vass, A.A. and Weston, A. (1990), Probation day centres as an alternative to custody: a 'Trojan horse' examined, *British Journal of Criminology*, 30: 189–206.

Von Hirsch, A. (1976) *Doing Justice*. New York: Hill and Wang.

Walker, M. and Beaumont, B. (1981) *Probation Work: Critical Theory and Practice*. Oxford: Blackwell.

Walker, N., Farrington, D. and Tucker, G. (1981) Reconviction rates of adult males after different sentences, *British Journal of Criminology* 21: 357–60.

Ward, K. (1979) Fuel debts and the probation service, *Probation Journal*, 26(4): 110–14.

Waterhouse, J. (1983) The effectiveness of probation supervision, in J. Lishman (ed.) *Social Work with Adult Offenders*, Research Highlights Number 5. Aberdeen: University of Aberdeen.

Way, T. (1932) Relaxations of standards of ordered life, *Probation*, 1(12): 187–8.

White, S. (1978) The nineteenth century origins of pre-sentence reports, *Australian and New Zealand Journal of Criminology*, 11: 157–78.

Whitehouse, P. (1983) Race, bias and social enquiry reports, *Probation Journal*, 30(2): 43–9.

Whitfield, D, (1997) *Tackling the Tag*. Winchester: Waterside.

Whitfield, D. (1998) *Introduction to the Probation Service*, 2nd edn. Winchester: Waterside.

Wilkins, L.T. (1958) A small comparative study of the results of probation, *British Journal of Delinquency* 8: 201–9.

Wilkinson, J. (1998) Developing the evidence-base for probation programmes. PhD thesis, University of Surrey.

Williams, B. (ed.) (1995) *Probation Values*. London: Ventura Press.

Williams, B. (1996) *Counselling in Criminal Justice*. Buckingham: Open University Press.

Williams, B. (1999) *Working with the Victims of Crime*. London: Jessica Kingsley.

Willis, A. (1983) The balance between care and control in probation: a research note, *British Journal of Social Work*, 13: 339–46.

Willis, C. (1983) *The Use, Effectiveness and Impact of Police Stop and Search Powers*. Home Office Research and Planning Unit Paper 15. London: Home Office.

Wilson, J.Q. and Kelling, G. (1982) Broken windows: the police and neighborhood safety, *Atlantic Monthly*, March: 29–38.

Woolf, Lord Justice (1991) *Prison Disturbances April 1990: Report of an Inquiry*, Cm. 456. London: HMSO.

Wootton, B. (1959) *Social Science and Pathology*. London: George Allen & Unwin Ltd.

Worrall, A. (1997) *Punishment in the Community*. London: Longman.

Worrall, A. (2000) What works at One Arm Point?, *Probation Journal*, 47: 243–9.

Wright, A. (1984) *The Day Centre in Probation Practice*, Social Work Monograph 22. Norwich: University of East Anglia.

Young, J. (1999) *The Exclusive Society. Social Exclusion and Difference in Late Modernity*. London: Sage.

Young, J. and Matthews, R. (eds) (1992) *Rethinking Criminology: The Realist Debate*. London: Sage.

Young, P. (1976) A sociological analysis of the early history of probation, *British Journal of Law and Society*, 3: 44–58.

Younghusband, E. (1954) Probation personnel, in *European Seminar on Probation*. New York: United Nations.

Zedner, L. and Lacey, N. (1995) Discourses of community, *Journal of Law and Society* 22: 301–25.

Index